101 Jewish Poems for the Third Millennium

101 JEWISH POEMS FOR THE THIRD MILLENNIUM

Edited by

Matthew E. Silverman
&
Nancy Naomi Carlson

 THE ASHLAND POETRY PRESS

Printed in the United States of America

ISBN: 978-0-912592-84-8

LCCN: 2019953780

Cover art: Jody Sachs

Cover design: Claire Zoghb

Contents

Yehoshua November

Foreword

As an undergraduate, I was fortunate to take a poetry course taught by Maria Mazziotti Gillan, a daughter of Italian Immigrants who grew up in the tenements of Paterson, New Jersey, during the 1940s and 50s. Gillan's poems often explore her adolescent struggle to shed the skin of her ancestors and assimilate into American culture. Ultimately, many of Gillan's poems come full circle and represent a reclaiming of her Italian roots. "The universal is in the particular," Gillan reiterated throughout the semester, not letting us forget one of the great writing axioms (I've since seen attributed to both Joyce and Chekhov): The counterintuitive secret to reaching the widest audience, to moving the most readers, lies in telling one individual's (often your own) idiosyncratic story with all its particular flavoring. Or stated differently, the mundane details that constitute a single life can tell a story much larger than themselves. Not surprisingly, despite my efforts to craft universal poems to be read for eternity—poems stripped of cultural and chronological specificity—my teacher encouraged me to write about my life as a traditional Jew in the contemporary world. I think, thematically—but also theologically—there was something very Jewish about Gillan's suggestion, especially when Judaism is considered in light of Midrashic and Chassidic teachings. Gillan's mantra also helps explain why poetry may serve as the ideal medium for achieving some of the goals of *101 Jewish Poems for the Third Millennium*.

But what are the goals of this anthology? In her Holocaust poem "Pines at Ponary," which appears toward the beginning of *101 Poems*, Ellen Bass writes about forest trees surrounding a mass grave: "Their leaves offered oxygen/ to victims and executioners, the same. / They drank moisture, blood, minerals. / Each year increasing another ring." I am told that, at least in part, *101 Jewish Poems for the Third Millennium* was borne out of a timely impulse to put Jewish themes front and center in an era seeing an alarming resurgence of anti-Semitism. (The recent synagogue shooting in my former hometown of Pittsburgh and another in San Diego provide two tragic examples.) In a sense, this anthology has assigned itself the ambitious goal of cautioning us not to remain oblivious, like the pines of Ponary, passing their time, indifferent to—in fact, nurtured by—an ugly and dangerous form of hatred. Indeed, this anthology does not let contemporary Americans forget the cruelty that took root last century, across the ocean. For it shows us, in the case of Matthew

Lippman's poem "Keeping Kosher," anti-Semitism simmers close to home; it might trail just behind the car of two unsuspecting Jewish teens "talking about the Beastie Boys" in suburban Maryland.

Despite including poems that address or reference the Holocaust, *101 Jewish Poems* is not a Holocaust anthology. Nor is it largely about anti-Semitism—directly. Like so many of the best contemporary poems, a number of works included here awaken us to a sanctity or beauty that pulses beneath the quotidian skin of daily life. In the case of this anthology, that daily life is informed—subtly or overtly—by Jewish identity and the particular shapes and forms it has assumed in the Third Millennium. In calling our attention to the idiosyncratic struggles and delights of ordinary people, poetry revives us from our habituation and restores a living and breathing humanity to its subjects, both of which are crucial in attempts to dampen hatred of any group seen as *Other*.

Leah Browning's "I Go Back in Time and Rescue My Mother" is one poem likely to do some of this work. Browning's speaker recalls her mother often announcing, "I just want to run away." A plea uttered when the strains of domesticity—"the whining, / bickering children, the unfulfilled ambitions… The loneliness. The emptiness"—push a parent to the threshold of what he or she can endure. Determined to save her mother from her disappointing life, the speaker travels back in time, enters her childhood home in the form of "a gust / of cold air, blowing in under the front door." "'I can save you,'" the gust of wind whispers, pulling the mother's hand toward the unlocked front door. To the speaker's surprise, however, her mother "slips away, turning instead toward the table," back to her uninspiring familial obligations. In this selfless moment, she has "squander[ed] what feels like her only chance for escape…" The narrative of a caregiver whose sacrifices we come to understand only much later—perhaps when we are called upon to make similar sacrifices ourselves, as Browning's poem goes on to illustrate—is a universal one. Browning's particular retelling reminds us of our shared struggles, vulnerability, and heroism.

Interestingly, the editors of this anthology have chosen to label the 101 poems that follow *101 Jewish Poems*. The choice calls to mind an old question: What constitutes a Jewish poem? This book—featuring poems by non-Jews who address Judaism directly alongside poems by Jews who, in some cases, make no mention of Judaism at all—complicates the question in both new and familiar ways. As the range of poems in this anthology implies, a single satisfactory definition of a Jewish poem will remain elusive. However, Browning's poem, like many of the pieces printed here, qualifies as Jewish not merely because it features a mother figure frying *latkes*, but because it also implies something central about Jewish spirituality: profound meaning resides not in a moment of transcendence but in the un-romanticized rigors of daily life. In this sense, the poem echoes the Midrashic theology which suggests the universe was created because "G-d desired a dwelling place in the lowest realm." Or, as the Chassidic mystics explain, earthly life—humanity's mundane or fragile moments—constitutes G-d's true home.

According to Chassidic thought, the metaphor of "home"—the place one is free to be oneself—is precise and instructive: that our world experiences no Divine light, in contrast to the Heavens, is not because G-d is absent. Rather, here—in the lower realm—G-d is simply His unknowable self. Here, in the everyday, a spiritual core beyond revelation resides. Or, said differently, the Divine remains concealed in the lower realm so that humanity may fill the open space with light—a feat achieved, for example, when Browning's mother figure encounters and withstands her particular lower realm challenge. It has always seemed to me that contemporary poets—many of whom identify as agnostics or atheists—intuit the "Dwelling Place in the Lowest Realm" theology, at least on a symbolic or secular level. For so many contemporary poets mine for meaning in the mundane—in the small particulars—when we might expect them to cast their gaze on larger transcendent truths. Contemporary poets are not fooled by the seeming absence of light in the everyday. They uncover and call our attention to the lower realm's inherent luminescence.

Perhaps an insistence that the sacred dwells in the ordinary also helps explain why the zany speaker in Joanna Fuhrman's poem—one of many pieces in this anthology that omit direct allusion to Judaism—confesses a crush on "chipped gold nail polish," "the number 8 bus," and "New Jersey pollution." Often, Chassidic thought emphasizes that what appears mundane or flawed holds a spark deriving from the highest spiritual source. In this vein, Fuhrman's poem brings some of the everyday particulars we may encounter in the "lower realm's" Third Millennium into sharp focus. Much of contemporary poetry—like Midrash and Chassdic thought—turns upside down the hierarchy of the sacred and the profane. It suggests the best place to find the Infinite is in the finite, and the best place to find the universal is in the particular.

An anthology concerned with Judaism and anti-Semitism must also broach the question of Jewish continuity. Some see the continued existence of the Jewish people—few in number but survivors of some of history's most powerful and pointed attacks—as a great mystery. Devout Jews will point to Biblical promises guaranteeing Divine protection. Cynics will point to the winds of happenstance. Yet others might cite a phenomenon the Jewish anthropologist and ethnographer Jonathan Boyarin once called "inescapable Jewishness." Naturally, as several pieces in *101 Jewish Poems* remind us, inescapabilty is most apparent when one desires to escape, to sever ties, but remains bound in the rope of his or her bittersweet Jewish inheritance. Take, for example, the conclusion of David Lehman's "Sabbath Feast." The poem's speaker—a man seemingly estranged, at least to some extent, from Jewish ritual life—reflects on his past: "How sweet to the man are the days of his youth. How surprised he would be, could he / hear his own voice clamoring for attention at the dinner table with his parents and sisters / and perhaps an uncle and aunt on a Friday night in 1961." "A Small Tribe," an Edward Hirsch poem that also appears in these pages, offers another example of inescapable Jewishness, concluding with the story of

> ... a daydreamer
> who bought a new hat
> every year for Passover
> so that he could stand outside
> the temple,
> which he refused to enter,
> though he loved the songs
> and wanted to be close
> to the prayers.

Jews have been adhering to and rebelling against Jewish texts and traditions for thousands of years. Though the two approaches may come across as diametrically opposed, both actions reflect a relationship to Judaism. For only a Jew can meaningfully embrace or throw off the yoke of Jewish tradition—much the same way only a child can disobey or listen to his or her parent. In fact, according to the Chassidic mystics, that one can disobey the Torah and be forgiven, make others and oneself cry and be forgiven, reflects a connection between humanity and the Divine that transcends the Torah—though, ironically, it's the Torah itself that tells us this secret. Perhaps this is what Philip Schultz hints at in his poem "Yom Kippur," titled after the Jewish holiday when ultimate forgiveness is said to be granted and one's essential Jewish spark shines forth. Or at least, according to Schultz, this is what Jewish tradition asks us to believe. That Schultz's speaker remains in doubt as to Yom Kippur's powers but still finds himself in the synagogue on the holiday provides another example of inescapable Jewishness. "Yom Kippur" tells us, among other things,

> ...To believe that no matter what
> you have done to yourself and others
> morning will come and the mountain
> of night will fade. To believe,

for these few precious moments
in the utter sweetness of your life.

This anthology also suggests Jewish continuity owes something to the kindness and sensitivity of non-Jewish neighbors in unlikely places. In Wendy Barker's "Waking Over *Call It Sleep*," the speaker of the poem, a non-Jewish English teacher in a city where only 1% of the population identifies as Jewish, attempts to teach Henry Roth's famous novel. She is rattled and unnerved—"shaking, after decades of holding forth in linoleum-floored classrooms"—when one of her students offers up an offensive comment about Jews. She then ponders a possibility less uncommon than we might think: Perhaps one of her students whose families hail from "Monterrey or Laredo" will learn, as one of her friends recently has, that he or she descends from ancestors who "came over from Spain to escape the Inquisition…" The poem implies a powerful lesson: in practicing baseless hatred, we may come to discover that, all the while, we have unknowingly hated our closest friends, our families, or even ourselves.

In his most recent collection, the Polish poet Adam Zagajewski dedicates a poem, "Ruth," to his neighbor, a recently deceased Holocaust survivor. The poem attempts to describe what it means to be a Jew. "It's simple and incomprehensible, like Algebra," Zagajewski writes. Clearly, it's not simple at all. Traditional Jewish Law, *Halacha*, says a Jew is an individual born to a Jewish mother. The Russian poet Marina Tsvetaeva famously said, "Every poet is a Jew." (In my experience, every Jew, however, is not a poet.) The word Jew derives from the name *Yehuda*, one of the twelve sons of Jacob and the father of one of the twelve tribes. In the Book of Esther, Mordechai—a member of the tribe of Benjamin and a Jewish hero in a time when Jewry faced annihilation at the hands of a terrible anti-Semite—is called a *Yehudi*. Why? The Talmud answers, "He was a Benjaminite. Yet he was called a *Yehudi* because he rejected idolatry—and anyone who rejects idolatry is called a *Yehudi*." The name Yehuda derives from the Hebrew word for thankfulness (a behavior exemplified in Carol V. Davis's poem "In the Scheme of Things"). Thus, the Talmud implies, to lack gratitude is a form of idolatry. According to Chassidic thought, the suggestion that G-d is not present in all places and all things, that anything exists independent of the Divine, also constitutes idolatry. Albeit largely in a secular fashion, contemporary poets so often assert profound meaning and sanctity in all things. And today's poets reveal there is much to be thankful for in the ordinary individuals and everyday phenomena we tend to overlook. Aren't all poets, then, at least symbolic *Yehudis*? Perhaps, the universal, our shared humanity, will shine forth through the particular voices in these poems and play a part in limiting the hatred that undermines peace in our Third Millennium.

Editors' Introduction

When we first began this project, we had one goal in mind: to bring together a collection of Jewish-themed poems representative of the Third Millennium. We wanted to include writers from many different walks of life: both Jewish and non-Jewish, secular and non-secular, known and emerging, as well as poets writing in other languages. We naively thought 40 to 50 poems would suffice, but we were flooded with over 800 poems in response to our call for submissions, and we quickly realized even 101 poems—"a small tribe," to borrow Ed Hirsch's words—gathered here are not enough to cover the wide range of thoughts and events that have occurred in the last 20 years. We could unfortunately not include every Jewish poet writing today, and we based our selections not only on the literary merit of each poem, but also on how well it contributed to the collection's goal of having diverse themes, voices, formats, and approaches to what is considered "Jewish-themed." This anthology is unique in that it contains several translations from such languages as Hebrew, Russian, and Spanish, and the majority of poems haven't been published before. The themes we eventually included in this collection range from traditional Jewish holidays, celebrations, and synagogue life, to more modern themes, such as same-sex marriage, disease-producing genes in Jewish carriers, and non-faith.

It did not take long to notice another pattern emerging, as readers may note as well. With anti-Semitism on the rise, we began to realize that the effect of the collection is not to define Judaism in a limiting way but to enable readers to see the depth of Jewish-related themes and their similarity to ideals and thoughts that affect any person living in this century.

A few words about the glossary. Some poets incorporated foreign words, mostly Hebrew and Yiddish, into their poems' universe by not italicizing them. Others chose to italicize them. We made the decision to define only the words the poets themselves had chosen to italicize in the text. We felt we had to respect each poet's choice, rather than consider which words we personally recognized or didn't. In some cases, the same words were spelled differently by different poets—understandable in that transliteration is not an exact science. *Chanukah*, for example, has many variant spellings, including *Chanuka*, *Hanukah*, *Hanuka*, and *Hanukka*. We were fortunate that most of the words that can't readily be found in an English dictionary or the internet were italicized, and hence can be found in our glossary.

Within these pages, we encourage you to savor and ruminate upon what the landscape of Jewish poetry and Jewish thought has become. While these poems both celebrate and honor Jewish traditions, they also reflect the human spirit that inhabits us all as members of the larger collective called Humanity.

Shalom

Marjorie Agosín

Entwined in Your Silence

Your room with the scent of sandalwood,
With a round table atop which sat the two silver candelabras
You would light for the Sabbath.

In that room
I learned to pray in another language,
Not to question the vast silences,
To allow the clear night wind
To play with the light of those candles
And emit their faint aroma.

Everything in you seemed far away.
You harbored within you impenetrable stories.
Entwined in your silence,
I learned not to question,
Only to understand.
We already knew the answers.

Translated from the Spanish by Alison Ridley

Patricia Averbach

My Father's Dream

The door is so low he bends to enter.
Inside, a woman is sitting at a table,
her hair wrapped in a yellow scarf.
As she invites him to sit down,
he sees her gold teeth flash.
She is unwrapping bundles bound
in old copies of *The Jewish News.*
The papers crumble in her hands,
small black letters, alephs, beits,
fall from the printed pages,
crawl across the floor like ants,
each bearing a message larger than itself.

The woman draws out skeins
of wool and lays them on the table.
She twists a length around her palm,
pulls out loops and lines
to weave an intricate cat's cradle.
Simple geometries appear, then
alphabets, and constellations.
"Do you know where you are?" she asks.
He shakes his head.
"Finland," she says,
pulling the strings tight.

There are no Jews in Finland.

What is he doing here?
He turns his eyes to the narrow door.
"Your turn," she says.

As he plucks the twisted strings
she hums an old niggun,
di di di die di di die dum

that hovers wordless in the air
and he remembers that his mother
di di die die di die die dum,
told him to meet her here.

Wendy Barker

Waking Over *Call It Sleep*

I'm the closest thing to Jewish in the class even though
at best I'm only one-eighth, according
    to my English mother, who insisted the shadowy figure
of her granny was a Jew since nobody knew
    her origins and everybody talked as if something had been
hushed up, shameful, and of course
    everything about her hawk-nosed face was unusually dark,
especially the ringlets of her unruly hair,
    or I suppose you could count the fact that I'm married
to a man whose grandparents arrived
    at Ellis Island from what is now Ukraine only three years
after Henry Roth, yet none of these
    students has the sekhl to know their teacher is a shiksa
and our group is as goyish as pork chops
    but they've all been children, and they love this novel,
they know what it's like to be
    speechless, powerless, afraid. Nobody needs me to explain
the terror of what lies beyond
    the front door and what lies within, and the paralysis
that comes from never knowing
    when to dash outside or stand by the window behind
the blinds. One year, while we were reading
    Ginsberg, I knew I'd have to describe Kaddish
though I'd never even heard it
    recited, but I gave it a go, saying in passing that only
1% of our city's population is Jewish
    which was when Heather quipped: "Of course, they're all
in Hollywood making millions from
    trashy movies." I put down my book and didn't move—you
could hear the whirr of the elevator
    down the hall. When I spoke, I said, "That was a very
offensive comment"—and I realized I was
    shaking, after decades of holding forth in linoleum-floored
classrooms. It wasn't like the times

I've heard someone saying wet, meaning wetback,
which are both despicable terms
        and I argue those too, but this time it was as though
I'd been slapped full in the face, called
        sheeny, kike, and I swear that tears came to my eyes
though I couldn't cry out "Gevalt, help,
        take that back, you ignorant little bitch." The tension lasted
beyond the ten-minute break, which
        I loosened to twenty, and not just for the smokers. This time
I've handed out maps that highlight
        Galicia, Brooklyn, Tysmenicz, the Lower East Side,
Avenue D, and 9th Street, and a list with
        explanations of terms: Passover, Ashkenazi, knish, shul,
and pogrom. We talk about Friday night
        and the candles, and everyone is right there in the room
with Roth and with me and with my
        husband who joins us after the break to tell about the author's
life with his duck farm and his goyish wife
        and his writer's block, and I begin to wonder if any of these
students with family from Monterrey or
        Laredo will someday learn—as a friend of mine did last year—
that a great-great-great-and-beyond
        grandfather came over from Spain to escape the Inquisition,
and if it will happen—as my friend Raul
        told me it did—that in the lighting of candles with relatives
gathered for a first Shabbat, an elderly aunt
        in the corner will begin to sigh and to weep, and when they
press her, ask her what's wrong,
        she'll tell them she's suddenly remembering an abuela who
covered her face with her hands
        every Friday night to greet the Divine, the Shechinah, and
who every week sent one grandchild
        to buy candles. A child, I'm thinking, who wore a silver
cross around her neck and had never
        heard *judía de mierda* hurled in her face with the auto-pilot
contempt of the six girls who chanted
        at me in the bathroom once during second grade, as they
pointed at the color of my striped
        dress: Blue, blue, you're a Jew, but I didn't get it—
I thought they were saying jewel.

Helen Bar-Lev

The Man on the Train

The man opposite me
on a filthy gloomy
subway train
is tall and young
small spectacles meet ears
and wavy black hair;
a beginning beard
creeps around his chin,
his skin is pale,
New Yorkers, after all,
do not see much of the sun;
he reads a newspaper
in Arabic

I sit thinking in Hebrew
of homecomings
and unforgiving conflicts –
above his head
three different warnings
of impending emergencies
this train could experience
which I read carefully,
given the circumstances

I am tempted to approach him
start a conversation,
there is a certain kinship after all,
a geographical connection –
I am not surprised when we alight
at the same station

He is spry and disappears
in a youthful instant
up the long flight of stairs

probably passing
the Israeli Rabbi
I have come to see

I ask the Rabbi about the Arab;
he is not impressed
Here in New York,
he tells me,
Jews and Arabs
always live
in the same
neighborhoods.

Dara Barnat

These Are the Sidewalks of Tel Aviv

—after "A Postcard From Tel Aviv" by Tuvia Ruebner

These are the bike lanes.
They're close to the sidewalks, be careful.
This is the square where someone
who cared about peace was killed.
They painted his footsteps black where he fell.
I push the stroller past them
every day. My son plays in the shadow
of peace. This is the city that holds me
as I sleep and as I lie awake.
People are out with their dogs at 3 a.m.
In this city, when I hear helicopters, I stop
what I'm doing. When you hear
more than one of them, it's serious.
I don't know why I keep returning
to this city that's never been
my own. Find me a place that speaks
my mother tongue.
Find me a home in Queens.
Find me a home in Manhattan.
Why Tel Aviv – hot all year, no rain
until December? Yet, I live
to feel those drops, to watch
the winter downpour from the window.
Is that why I've returned
(again), because Tel Aviv keeps me
waiting? This is the city
I run towards, then from, then towards,
and still from. No matter how
many times I walk the streets, they feel foreign.
Brodetsky. Zeitlin. Ibn Gvirol.
When I drive, though, I don't have to think
about where I'm going. My body
knows where to turn,

which intersections to avoid.
Maybe I hold on to Tel Aviv,
because this is the city that wrote me
my first poems, in a language
it doesn't know very well. Graffiti
in English is often misspelled.
The mesiah is coming.
I doubt the messiah is coming.
Tel Aviv doesn't care enough.
Tel Aviv cares about vegetables
from the *shuk*, perfect tomatoes.
Perfect pita and hummus. Green olives
for my son. Tel Aviv cares
about cold coffee and museums.
Here's the white sand on the beach.
Here's the Mediterranean Sea.
I've stood there alone, in the early morning.
The water changes by the hour.

Aliki Barnstone

Name Change

It was my grandfather's idea to change
the family name from Bornstein,
meaning *amber*
             or *burning stone* in German,
to Barnstone, also meaning *amber.*

In 1912, he, his father, stepmother,
and all his siblings stood before a judge
in Auburn, Maine,
             and Anglicized the vowels
within their name's consonants to conceal
being Jews within their souls and behind the walls
of home.
         (Shades drawn to hide Shabbat candlelight.)
The gems' classical name was *electron,*
"beaming sun," yet the Heliades' grief
made them poplars and their tears golden amber.

Two centuries before, the Emperor
Joseph the Second decreed that all Jews
immediately abandon
            Hebrew names
and adopt a constant German surname.
Tax them and keep track of them like the rest
of Christendom,
            except keep the Jews humble.
No Jew may take the surname of a noble
or renowned family.
           No Jew may keep
a name if someone complains it was his.

All circumcision books and all birth books
will be in German forever and ever.

The Jews will be registered, just as Jesus
was born in Bethlehem,
                              city of David,
where Joseph and Mary traveled to sign
the census decreed by Caesar Augustus.
Did the ancestors know the parallel—
register to be taxed (and rounded up later)—
when they chose lovely names: apple or pear
tree, rose, gold leaf, green field, or blooming valley?

My jeweler Zaide was a great magician
with diamonds, so I am told.
                              What if
in 1788, our ancestors
had been able to afford *Diamond*—
the hardest stone, dispersing spectral color—
would my grandfather have heard the brilliant name
as Jewish?
          and would he have chosen for us
Davies, Day, or even plain Smith instead?

Every time I look down at my left hand,
I behold
          the ring he gave my grandmother:
a platinum setting shaping a sun.
The diamond conceals
                    fire within
until, awakened by rays, it bursts
into rainbows and stars scattered on the walls
all around me:
                    the covenant with Noah:
God will never annihilate us again.

Tony Barnstone

American Spoken Here

The list came knocking on my door, wanting to know my name.
The list wanted to know from whence I came.
The list was making a list of foreign words, like *Pajama* and *Impala*.
The list planned to send them back to the *Boondocks*.
The list suspected that *Jasmine* was a *Thug* and *Cotton* an *Assassin*.

It started to get bad when they euthanized the alien animals at the zoo:
        Jackals and *Tigers*, *Cheetahs* and *Panthers*, too. And the *Cockatoos*.
Then the list set long nets to keep the *Tilapia* off our shores.
Soon they sent squads to the schools, swinging big sticks, seizing *Lollipops*
        and *Yo-yos*.
Now the list has posted rules in the shop windows: No *Guitars*. No
        Tambourines. Pot sold here, but not *Hashish*. And no more *Burkas*.

The list came to our house searching for foreign foods, *Hummus, Couscous, and*
        Baba Ghanoush. I was eating breakfast and the list said, "That is my
        Yoghurt" and took it from my hand. And then our *Chocolate* and our
        Sherbet. Everything we had. The list took everything. We didn't have
        anything left.

We had a large courtyard and all the children were playing ball. And an officer was
        also there. He said to my parents — my father had returned by then from
        fighting overseas — he then said:"You need to leave." And we were afraid.

Last night I saw the neighbors standing around pouring *Alcohol* on a burning
        pile of *Almanacs* and *Alfalfa* and stirring it with sticks.
The chemists are hiding their *Borax*, the jewelers are burying their *Platinum*
        and *Beryl*, the math teachers avoid Arabic numerals, and *Algebra*, and
        Algorithms.
And you have to watch your words. The German and French ones are okay.
But the list has its eye on *Soda*. And *Khaki*. And *Buggering*.

We had to disappear. Otherwise they would have taken us. I remember the
    day I found my neighbors gone and the door was swinging open. I
    walked into the kitchen and the floor was painted red with blood.

The list has its supporters, and they have a message for us: Dispose of the
    Roses! Uproot the *Tulips*! Blackjack that *Lilac*!
They want to count down from eleven million without using *Zero*.
They want to erase and erase until the page is pure white.

Move on, move on, there's nothing to see.

When you see the list on the street, it's best not to look right or left. Just
    keeping walking forward, eyes before your feet.

Ellen Bass

Pines at Ponary

*—100,000 people were murdered by the Nazis at Ponary,
10km southwest of Vilnius where my grandmother was born.*

Today is gray, drizzling,
but not enough for drops to pool
on the tips of the silver needles
or soak the bark of the pines at Ponary—
some of them
more than a century old. Here, when
the trains wheeled on numb
rails. And before I have gone
ten feet into the forest, I hear the sound.
Of course. There would have to be a train.
But I hadn't expected it still to run
like this, people
getting off and on with their packages.
I hadn't thought of the scent of resin spilling
into the cold afternoon. The trees
step to the rim
of the pits where Jews were shot
so the bodies fell in
efficiently. Their branches could save
no one. Their leaves offered oxygen
to victims and executioners, the same.
They drank moisture,
blood, minerals.
Each year increasing another ring.

Dan Bellm

Counting

What
if I
this moment
were only prayer,
not a thought or word
of one, nor even an
intention; sunlight on grass,
nothing of itself but what it
shows, or a bird that has called out, filled
with purest hearing; well, I have the prayers
in the book, and once again I have lost my
place, dreaming even past the prayer that calls on me
to listen up; must I start it all over, and where
would I begin; how far into the past would I unwind,
how far would a self have to cast itself out before it flew
beyond its reaches, to live, instead of being only lived in;
oh it's like asking to stop breathing; in the time I've spent worrying
the sun turned all to shadow, it began to rain, the scent of the mown grass
lifted into the trees, and now the light and shade have returned to their places
a little further on, in accordance with the number of moments that have passed.

15

Rabbi Hiyyah, called the Great, once said, *I have never in my life prayed with intention.*
One time I tried to intend, but only wondered in my heart whether I would be received
before the king, or sent into exile. How was I to know? This, of course, started the other
rabbis talking; Rabbi Samuel admitted, with a shrug, *I have been counting chickens;* Rabbi
Bun the son of Hiyyah said, *I have been counting the layers of stone in the wall,* and his eyes lit up
with this woeful confession; Rabbi Mattaniah sighed, since there is always one who feels responsible
for the prayers of all the rest, *Then let there be blessings on our heads, for I have noticed that whenever we come*
to the last of the benedictions, at which we are commanded to bow down, our heads are bowed of their own accord.
But look, I must have nodded off again, enumerating, losing track of what I meant to praise, drool on my shirt, or
else have had a dream, with none to interpret it; will You not look away from me awhile, as Job cried out, and let me be,
whilst I swallow my own spit? The rain has started falling again, even in the path of the sun, as if there's no reason to
decide which will be first or last, and a great round of song is circling among the uppermost branches of the spruces. Return to
me, O God, and I'll return, letting the day begin again even if it's halfway gone, extolling the One who removes the sleep from
my eyes, the slumber from my eyelids, and gives the rooster discernment to tell day from night; let me count the threads of You that I might tug at,
complicated by being many, simple by being one, and if not to arrive at wanting nothing, which is another desire, then to
yearn for what is given, including the dust and the ash, and the last moment You have counted up for me, wherefore I clap my hand unto my mouth.

Jill Bialosky

They Came

—for the families of the deceased buried in Jewish Cemeteries desecrated since January of 2017

They came with small rocks
and pebbles to place on the holy ground
where gravestones had been turned over and desecrated.
They came with their relative's plot number
scribbled on scraps of paper.
They came with tears in their eyes,
they came with their memories and
grief unfurling like the sails of a ship
meeting the wind of the never-to-be-forgotten.
They came to see
what the destroyers had done,
granite and marble slabs with
the names and dates of the beloved
toppled as if the gravestones were bodies
with faces thrust into the mud.
They came to see whether there
was blood on the stones from
the hands of the destroyers.
They came and they remembered:
the hieroglyphics
of Hebrew; the red blossoms
of shame. They came
with fear in their eyes,
and horror in their throats.
They came with the foreknowledge
of evil dictators spewing caustic
rhetoric, red swastikas on the navy sleeves
of lieutenants, the sound of shrill
whistles, climbing wildflowers creeping up barbed wire,
Jewish stars cut from yellow fabric sewn
over the hearts of tattered coats.
They came to mourn
the Anniversary of the Apocalypse.

The sound of the nightingales, the scrolls
unwinding. They came to never forget
the possibility of extinction, the power
of a regime, the cowering of a populace.
They came and they
remembered too the collapse of
towers, the scouring of the pit,
the terrible blue skies,
the day in which the innocent
were forsaken.

Linda Blachman

Sarah Unbound

—*inspired by Aviva Gottlieb Zornberg's* The Beginning of Desire

When Sarah learned of
the burnt offering
the world fell off its axis

Her husband's arm, knife in hand
the altar, ropes binding tender
flesh, her son's stricken face, the wood,
the ram, her torn vision, shattered plans
fragments
spinning round her head
whirling waves of vertigo

She couldn't breathe
couldn't think
couldn't find her feet on the fissured earth
couldn't bear her splintered certainties
her son, her son, lost to her, almost lost to her
she became the shofar's anguished wail
breaking her into pieces
howling her into the vortex
where she willed her soul to fly away

Pity it happened eons before
meclizine and Klonapin
before Peter Levine woke the tiger and
world to trauma
before EMDR, SE, EFT
neurofeedback and neuroscience
before guardrails at the Golden Gate
before metta became medicine

Too late for my own mother
who followed the call of her angry God

to endless grief and shame
meekly trailed the blinkered doctors
to their altar of straps and shocks

She lay down with trembling trust
awoke with empty eyes
knew the abyss, curled her toes around the edge
didn't jump but never lived

No stranger to vertigo's curse myself
another link in trauma's long chain
stretching back to you Sarah *emeinu*
mother of my mother
of all mothers who tiptoe towards the pit
in garments of sackcloth and ash
heads bowed, bodies debased
children torn from arms
hope slashed, dreams dashed

Shim'i! Sarah, listen to me
I am only 75 to your 127 but
I've learned a thing or two
from my advantaged perch
in time

Nothing is worse than that scream
inside you when you cannot
protect your child
but, Sarah, you must hang on
help is coming
late though it is

You're still in shock
there is no blame
trauma seizes the brain
freezes vision, cognition, action

Hagar the slave you banished to the desert with her son
couldn't see the well through her weeping
the battered wife sees the open door and cannot move
frozen, you saw only the whirlwind
and the cave

Your mind won't help you now, Sarah
ground yourself in grief
ground yourself in the body
breathe through your pain
thaw your tears, mourn all you've lost
a better land awaits you

Plant your feet on the parched earth
sink roots into soil watered with
your sisters' sorrow
deepen yourself
have *rachmones* upon yourself
soften, Sarah, soften
we are all connected
you are not alone

Your grieving may never be done
but right now, Sarah, look up, look up
t'rei, see what remains
wipe the tears that cloud your vision
anchor yourself in the present moment

Behold
the trees, the river, your hands
your beating heart
a bird sings
can you hear it?
you're alive!
can you feel it?

Raise your eyes and see
your son. Your child lives!
see his frenzied eyes searching for some
ground of being, a mirror

Do not turn away
from your wounded child, defiled
reminder of all you have lost
find your mother's heart in *his* need
fix him in your sights
let him be the lighthouse
beaming your way back from the pit

Negate the negation, Sarah
choose life so Isaac, your only born
your miracle baby
can find himself in your
loving eyes
and won't live out his days half-blind
groping for walls
in your darkened tent

Your child calls, Sarah. *Afoh at, Ema?*
where are you, my mother?
find your *hineni* for him, for yourself
I am here, my son, my child
I am here!

Honor yourself, our mother, our own
rise up to your full stature
remember that you are remembered
remember delight
remember yourself
redeem the shining soul
with which you were born

As strength returns
perspective helps, *Emeinu*
we're all lost and found and lost again
in history's wilderness
no one is perfect, nothing is certain
we have limited power, limited control

Still, the pillar of fire guides by night, by day
the pillar of cloud brings renewing rain
healing is possible

Sarah, we want you to heal
Through the bleating shofar's cry
we are calling you to return to us
Creation is not done
and a mother is needed!

Three thousand eight hundred years
since you left us, another Temple burns
in a faraway land promised to the tired and poor
another Nero fiddles on his gilded throne while
babies torn from parents' arms wail their terror in urban cages
empty-armed mothers howling their helplessness
fathers falling off the earth in despair
safe places of learning becoming prisons
teaching what no child should learn
the language of funerals, AR-15s, SKS rifles
those are guns, Sarah
we have found efficient ways to kill
our young

So much has changed so little has changed
everyone connected by wires and screens
everyone falling off the Tower of Babel
we are drowning in things but thirsting
for mater   matter   Mother

Shim'i! Sarah, hold your ground
we are all your children
and require a late-in-life miracle
one we will seed together in your ancient womb
we need you
returned to us, reborn
swollen with life
ready to labor

Our Mother of pillowy breast, muscle and mercy
          of feet hugging the earth, arms clasping the world
          push us beyond the wheel of suffering
          to birth a vision, a true and new beginning

Wise compassionate Mother
          mend our world with kindness
          help us love our neighbor
          walk us gently on the regenerative earth
          purify our hearts, teach us how to pray
          make us messengers of hope
          strengthen our resolve

move us to right action
show us how to rest

Sarah *emeinu*, we want you to sing again
long green notes
we want your full-throated laugh
laced with skepticism, intelligence and joy

Rock your children with new songs —
lullabies at twilight, rising protests at dawn —
gather the scattered notes of your dirge
lay them tenderly on the black cloth
heed Rebbe Nachman's teaching
to join white dots of goodness to white dots
transforming dissonance into coherence
lamentation into the long lyrical line
of gladness and praise, the unbroken
Tekiah Gedolah

Embrace it all, Sarah
we are returning to the river
and this time need to cross
we are all needed and we need each other
we need a once-upon-a-time to believe in
where you, Hagar, Avraham, Ishmael, Yitzchak
and all your children's children coexist
in a peaceable kingdom
sitting by the river, every home secure
every home flanked by olive trees

With all my heart, this I believe
a new song is coming, a new story

Love is coming, Sarah
the best weapon against terror

And the generations are waiting.

Michele Bombardier

I Dream I Understand My
Great-Grandmother's Yiddish

—Makht zikh greyt tzu antloyfn.

What is heaviness
but the weight of fear,
the sound of advancing hooves,
the noose of the village circled,
the pull of wagon into woods.
What is memory
but a hat you cannot take off.
What is survival
but a monkey who climbs
and climbs up your body
until you become tree.
The monkey grabs
into your upper reaches,
pulls itself to safety,
makes a home.
When you feel your scalp tingle,
Bubelah, it's only monkeys in your hair.
Sometimes the monkey climbs down,
holds out the hat,
shakes it. Sometimes
you are not a tree,
but prey. Listen.
They are coming.
Makht zikh greyt tzu antloyfn:
Get ready to run.

Bruce Bond

Benthos

The fathoms take what we know of light,
the ache of it that dims as it goes
cold, deeper into the ache of dark.

Down here an eye is its own lantern,
sunk among the cuttlefish and squid,
the angel flesh that swims among the wreckage.

Today I walked into a small museum.
On a wall, a hill of spectacles,
teeth, a memoir bound in human skin.

I have read this book, skin to skin,
and yet I think a part of me reads it
in the dark. If this is the past,

it is far too tiny and too enormous.
What you make out in the many faces
gets lost in the unspeakable focus

of one. And each one difficult to name,
to recognize now, beneath the mask
of no mask. Not enough food to live,

and too much to die. That's what they say.
And it goes on that way for a while,
until the story of the boy who begs

to be shot. The core of us is strange.
Bones of faces float to the surface.
And deeper still, a voice, neither theirs

nor ours. Like a heavy net of cautions
that binds us to a world. Perhaps a prayer,
a memoir's future tense, or the last

breath of a man, here, high above the dark
floor, above the drowned, as we know them,
the gas blue eel, our black and silent stars.

Pia Borsheim

Sanctuary

Shabbat Shirah and we twelve women gather
at the sea. We pray, sing, and laugh together,
cook up old tales and soup, add just enough
spice to keep the tongue wanting more.

Large-breasted, large-hearted, we hear each
other's sorrows as the ocean licks the shore.
We chop onions, sauté the mushrooms,
braise the meat of friendship, sink our teeth
into the chicken bone, its juicy flesh no less
delicious than our own.

Stay a while. Rock in this chair.
Look out over pelicans and dolphins
who swoop and dive, swoop and dive,
their fins and feathers swelling in salt
air. Let me breathe this holy union
all the days of my life. May we scatter
home to unite again, our pursuers
vanquished, we grains of sand,
we stars in the sky.

Leah Browning

I Go Back in Time and Rescue My Mother

I know just where to find her, standing at the stove,
frying potato latkes in a cast-iron skillet. Her apron
is spattered with dark spots of grease, and waves
of heat rise up from the stove, pasting her dark hair
against the dampness of her neck and temples.

"Can't you make them any faster?" I am asking,
ten years old, at the table with my brother and sister.
The little pancakes are made of raw potato, grated
into a bowl and mixed with egg and salt and pepper.

It is dark outside, early winter. I arrive as a gust
of cold air, blowing in under the front door, hovering
in the space over the table, over the serving plate
with its bed of paper towels to absorb the excess oil.

There have been so many times that she's said,
"I just want to run away," spoken in anger
and in desperation, that I expect her to come
willingly, to take the ghostly fingers I offer
and allow herself to be pulled away

from all of us, from that life—the whining,
bickering children, the unfulfilled ambitions,
the husband who works long hours and listens
from a distance. The loneliness. The emptiness.

Everything that I know now she must have felt.
"I can save you," I whisper, pulling at her hand,
but she slips away, turning instead toward the table,
squandering what feels like her only chance for escape,

though the door is unlocked and she's chosen a million
times to stay. So I seep out of my childhood

home and go back to my own life. To the whining,
bickering children, the unfulfilled ambitions,
the husband who works long hours and listens

from a distance. The loneliness. The emptiness.
My mother calls on weekends after going
to bookstores or concerts, after sleeping until ten.
I stand at the stove, cooking hot foods over cast iron.

When my daughter arrives from her future life
to save us both, I find that I scarcely feel the hint
of air on my hand. But I am ready. I've been waiting
years now for someone to come and rescue me.

She pulls my arm away from the clothes I am folding,
from the dirty dishes and the trash that needs to go out.
And we get all the way to the front door before I hear
her voice—nine and a half years old, siren sweet rising
up the stairs—and find that I, too, am unable to leave.

Nancy Naomi Carlson

My Goyishe Ex-husband

For eighteen years he was one of the chosen
to help knead the challah dough:
yeast and sugar dissolved in a tepid bath,
oil mixed with eggs, flour sifted on top.
Flour dusted his hands like pollen,

like ash—what we might have buried
if given the chance, before our baby,
born blue but alive, was whisked away
and we, not knowing to question
Jewish law—*halacha*—our son deemed

"stillborn" for not having lived out a month.
A mishap of DNA was to blame,
though what were the odds
that our bloods—mine Ashkenazic, and his
from a Swedish coast, would carry

the same mutant gene?
We could not keep grief from our home
or from sticking to skin,
unlike the dough whose lumps we tried to best—
a pinch of flour one at a time—

so it could rise, become more than itself,
to be rolled into ropes of three or six,
then braided like hair of the Sabbath Queen
and left to rise again on a parchment tray,
before baked to a perfect gold.

Doritt Carroll

the Jew i used to be

believed the light
looked different on Rosh
Hashanah

the Jew i used to be
thought the angels really
did look down

although they never cared
what they
saw

that long ago girl whose
teeth gapped
in a jack-o'-lantern
smile

thought the autumn air
smelled holy
if holy meant rotting leaves
with a shot of gin

watched the shadows of bare
branches
write a scripture on the
sidewalk

thought the slats of golden
light
were a picket
fence

holding us in our
pen
of otherness

Laura Cesarco Eglin

That's It

If I take the accent off cáncer
I shift the emphasis
toward its exit, I try
to tell her that this is not the end of the line

But I know that going from serious to severe
the pain comes to point out there it is,
the word, what accent does it have?
In which language does it hurt less?

At thirty, history is heavier
in my body your cancer, and yours
and hers, and his tell
in me, the family is clearly marked

A mammogram, an ultrasound
after palpating a nodule
makes everything more real. They tell me
to my face: cancer

I learned right away what it meant so I wouldn't
be afraid to say it, with all
its letters, the expression in my mouth
exceeds my mere words

I stretch my mouth horizontally and the cancer
is operated on in the United States
I include my nose in these growths and I say
cáncer or I touch your סרטן in my memory

hoping to dispel it with my tongue
spit it out, out of superstition
my body, mine, I speak it, I say it
I'm here, it doesn't end here.

Translated from the Spanish by Scott Spanbauer

33

Stephen Cramer

Water

1941: another pastor, taken prisoner,
was made to spit on his beloved

scriptures: spit, turn the page,
spit, turn the page, & this

not once or twice but for hours.
& when his mouth had given all

it could offer, the wells beneath
his tongue gone dry as a page,

the attending soldier generously
bent to him & spit in his mouth

so that he could continue,
the pastor's mouth become a chalice

not for holy words but
for rage. But something happened then

that the soldier did not expect:
at the moment it was bathed in saliva,

the scroll remembered its scroll's past
as a tree—chapter & verse gone back

to the annulated core of heartwood.
It hadn't even known how much

it had missed the rain, the clench
of roots around a dying spring.

It's written that the scripture is *a well*
of living waters, but really it's just

a dry old leaf, cut off from its source
until it becomes moist & supple

in our cells. So whatever sacrilege
the pastor felt, whatever dim victory

the soldier reveled in, the pastor
wasn't spitting on the scripture,

because the scripture was in his chest,
in his tongue. He *contained* it,

& it cascaded through him
the way that our bodies

are how water evolved to walk around
when it's not coursing down a river.

Carol V. Davis

In the Scheme of Things

The roof is leaking
through a light fixture

Grateful for rain after a scorched summer

My daughter has not called for months
texts unanswered I want to send again and again

She gives away all she has, collects food to distribute

A bill for $450   Did we leave the lights on all night?
Use more than our allotment of water?

We both have jobs, paychecks

The new cat has disappeared
how can I tell its former owner?

My husband's spine is behaving

Rosh Hoshanah, I break open a pomegranate
spill its seeds over the counter, swoop them into my palm

their juice runs through my fingers

Staining red everywhere it flows

Charles Dobzynski

Everything's Just Fine

I send my lookout eye out as a scout
in the rubbish-dump of the stars
Everything's fine he declares   the universe
continues to expand like stretched plastic
here and there a few quasars are quarrelling
galaxies cut classes
black holes take up dealing in contraband colors
Space refuses to bow and kowtow
and would rather stand with its back against the tape-measure
Time attends to milking the cow
a few rebellious stars have graffitied the night
But apart from that, under the awning and under the drainpipe
          Everything's just fine

I send my inquiring hand on patrol
as a rover
in movie-houses airports shops
and supermarkets
Everything's fine, she declares, there are crowds
consumption has become an Olympic sport
the banks are schools of whales
the media blather the same globalized slang
They buy GMOs and DVDs and dividends
trinkets and trick packages
The sales figures are soaring for begging bowls
for condoms for carbon dioxide
Hospitals are swollen up to the operating room
Newspapers and TV screens make blood donations
by way of murders and assassinations
They give out steroids at the State Employment Service
But apart from that, under the awning and on the litter
          Everything's just fine

I give my dissolute ear a green light
Under the trees in the hedges and flowerbeds
The trees are dying, she declares
Burning bushes auction off their ashes
The flowerbeds are reserved for mass graves
of a planned apocalypse
To protect them from the heat-wave
they've sent the elderly to arctic clubs
to sit on the melting ice-floes
But apart from that, under the awning and under the skylight
        Everything's fine   Everything's just fine

Translated from the French by Marilyn Hacker

Sharon Dolin

If I Told You

If I told you I am Roma, if I told you I am named
after my great-grandmother Sabina and that
Sabina is a gypsy name, if I told you
there is no DNA marker for Roma but I believe

my people are Jewish Roma. If I told you
I feel Roma in my blood when I watch flamenco
and I have a common Roma blood type,
if I know how to speak every Romance language

but Romanian and my Romanian-American grandmother
who knew no Yiddish knew how to say
Cum va place? How do you like it? in Romanian.
If I told you that proves nothing and everything.
If I told you I am related to a Hollywood gangster
on my Romanian side and you probably believe

gypsies are gangster thieves. If I told you I am a thief
and I am stealing my Roma identity, if I have never begged
for a coin never sat outside a subway or train station
though once, stranded in Boston, asked strangers

for a bed, ended up on a bench in the police station.
If I told you I slept in a tent or under the canopy
of stars like a wandering Jew or gypsy,
if the rhythms of my clapping are Roma

and my people are from Iasi
in Moldovia in eastern Romania, if I told you
Roma played at Jewish weddings and Jews
played at Roma weddings, and during
the Iasi pogrom of June, 1941, Romani were caught
laughing as they helped the Nazis. If this is when

I have my doubts about being Roma.
If I told you the Romani part of me believes
only in song and the Jewish part insists
on writing it down. If I told you

some Romani have light eyes and hair like mine.
If I told you the part of me that wanders is a gypsy Jew
and that part of me never feels at home. That being
an outcast once, why not be an outcast twice.

Moshe Dor

Reflections

Stars are the eyes of God.
           —Louise Erdrich

If stars are the eyes of God
He must have shifted His gaze
away from His unfortunate world
or shut His eyes in disgust; but I
prefer to believe that God is blind
and throughout this vast universe
stars merely reflect random light.

Translated from the Hebrew by Barbara Goldberg

Erika Dreifus

The Price of Lilith's Freedom

Adam complained before God that the wife He had given him had deserted him, and God sent forth three angels to capture her. They found her in the Red Sea, and they sought to make her go back with the threat that, unless she went, she would lose a hundred of her demon children daily by death. But Lilith preferred this punishment to living with Adam.
   —excerpted from Louis Ginzberg, *The Legends of the Jews* (Volume 1; trans.
    Henrietta Szold)

The deal was this:
liberation from our unequal coupling
and the ability to spring free from his authority.
In exchange, he gets the house,
where, in time, he'll live with another
and raise a family.
I must travel far, far away.
Each day will bring fresh spasms:
pain, loss, grief—
all to be borne alone.
The deal was this.
And as unbearable as it sounds:
pain, loss, grief—
to be borne,
I repeat,
far away, and alone—
I'd take that deal again.
Any day.

David Ebenbach

While They Choose a New Pope, I Eat a Bagel

These are old occupations. In Vatican City there is no
wi-fi, not until after they've sent their white smoke
rising. Black smoke means they're still at it. Here
it would mean the bagel's burning. There's no white kind.
They used to carry them around on sticks, which is why
the hole in the middle, and we keep it even though
sometimes the butter ends up pooling right in the center
of the plate. We keep things the way they are.
The Cardinals—do they sit around a table, a dark table
older than America? They may have bagels of their own,
though it's hard to imagine them licking cream cheese
off their thumbs. But things do change. They used to
lock the bishops in the chapel until they got it done, and now
there are hotels and buses. They wake up to a coffee maker,
maybe a continental breakfast. And I've got a toaster,
and a food processor to make the hummus, everything
I need. There may be windows high up in the wall,
shuttered. Nobody's allowed to see things in process.
The Cardinals crowd around, one of them almost a Pope. Me,
I'm already eating the bagel.

Dina Elenbogen

A Voice

In the beginning   a whimper
Pounding of heart-steps
Whispers of open fists
Prayer notes in stone

Pounding of heart-steps
Chirps of morning songs
Prayer notes in stone
The language of angels

Chirps of morning songs
A girl stands at the threshold
Hears the language of angels
Her own music breaking

A girl-woman stands at the threshold
Chants the first words of Torah
Her own voice breaking
Into stones with burning names

When a woman chants the first words
She finds inside her own voice
Stones with burning names
A cry becomes a scream

She finds inside her own voice
A silence   a sigh   an exaltation
A cry becomes a scream
A song of abundance

A silence   a sigh   an exaltation
When a woman reaches the highest note
In her abundant song
Even the stones begin to tremble.

Eli Eliahu

Underground

And how can I help it
if the operation was successful and Baghdad
died, and nothing is left
but the music my father
would listen to on the stations of shame
while waiting in the underground parking lot
to drive me to the people's army
on his way to work.

And I will never forget
the sadness of his hand fumbling
for the Hebrew, to quickly switch
before we'd leave and emerge
above ground.

Translated from the Hebrew by Marcela Sulak

Julie R. Enszer

Niddah

I imagine being *frum*
but still with my wife
an Orthodyke
(though the fantasy
falls apart since
she isn't Jewish
but if she were)
I imagine us
following family
purity laws
niddah in Hebrew
the days of our menses
and seven days after —
seven clean days —
we sleep apart
I imagine some months
we might separate
three weeks counting
days waiting for
our reunion.

Here is the question
to which always I return:
I know G-d accounted
for our love
for the desire of
one woman for another
for families arranged
around lesbian
love lesbian desire
lesbian commitment
but still I wonder,
Did G-d account

for our bleeding
bodies when laying
the laws of niddah?

Pamela Epps

Blessings

Your hand is heavy
on my head. I have waited
my turn and stepped forward.
Your arm extends, palm down,
eyes shut, whispering a prayer.

This is my favorite part of the visit.
Otherwise I hardly see you.
You are either in synagogue
or searching your books as if
they held life's recipes for good luck.

Mostly my arms are folded in front of me
all weekend. But much younger I held
your fervor to my heart,
still missing you fiercely.

Now I have learned the sharp edge
of loss and care for just this small thing:
the feel of your big-knuckled hand on my head,
how this weight keeps me from floating away.

You have had five more children.
My older sister, your first,
has become a feminist.
I am fast on her trail. Ashamed,
I still want the blessing.
From a man who thanks god everyday
that he was not born a woman.

Forty years and one stroke later
you speak no known language.
You are asking me a question
that I pretend to understand.

I tell you I don't take solace in God,
that I have not learned how to pray.
My lips press your forehead.
I mumble a few words.
It could be a blessing.

Maia Evrona

Chanukah

During the years of my illness
I would forget all eight nights
in which direction the candles were placed
and in which to set them alight;
Was it right to left or left to right?

The fumes from the struck match
made my head ache. The yellow flames
above thin candles, fluttering like flags,
burned my eyes—always drawn
to what was then the painful bright.

Fatigued and easily mesmerized, I'd stare
as the blue wax dripped down the brass
menorah, like blue vines growing backwards,
until someone blew the shrinking candles out,
those fire hazards.

Andrew Field

The House of Rashi's Mind

A word, a single word,
the sound of it, and
through the sound, bleeding
through it, the multifaceted
meanings – these things
explode softly
in Rashi's mind,
wherein contains whole
landscapes of language,
orchards of meaning,
meadows of letters, all waiting
for the light of Rashi's mind
to illuminate
each pear tree, each flower.
He would read a sentence,
but what he sees
beneath the words
are worlds:
the whole ocean,
but also the color of the light
falling on the water
on a particular day.
Like a painter, he could recall
each color in his memory,
each figure, each drama,
and then evaluate a portion here,
there, and make the whole thing cohere.
This memory is like an enormous house,
with each room lit
by a thousand candles.
Entering the house,
we are aware of a book
turned into a starry sky,
which Rashi uses as a compass,
to navigate the bewildering world.

Hilene Flanzbaum

Separation

God said, "Let there be an expanse in the midst of water, that it may separate water from water."
—Genesis 1. 6

The Bible warns that a mother's portion
is suffering. Witness Eve who discovered
that Cain had murdered his brother; Lot's wife
who turned to salt in order to see her
daughters one last time. Stories of our ancestors
tell us what bearing a child will bring.
The very earth abets separation.
In the book of Genesis, chaos cleaves

unto the light and the dark: the firmament
and the waters. At the altar Isaac
feels his father's knife at his throat and learns
to flee. By violence, tenderness or mercy,
a child is severed from you, despite
what you want—because of what you want.

Diane Frank

Year of Opposites

Everyone gets into the truck. Also the goat.
     We have hay for the goat,
          a watermelon to slice for everyone else.
Everyone is dancing barefoot in Tiberius,
     watching the tourists baptize one another
          in the Jordan River.
Everyone is hoping a bomb won't go off
     when they visit Jerusalem—
          by the Wall or in a café
               in toss distance from
                    a palm-sized stone or a molotov cocktail.

Those days I was working with the gardener
     who spoke fluent Hebrew, Arabic and English
          at Kibbutz Yachad in the Northern Galilee.
It was better than working in the kitchen,
     where the cook, who only spoke Hebrew,
          would point to a huge pile of cucumbers,
             and say, *Green. Wash.*
Or a stack of red peppers—
     Red. Wash.
          Or a sink full of pots.
             Wash.

I spoke Hebrew with the Palestinian taxi driver
     who didn't know English.
He called the place I asked him to drive me
     Sof Olam – end of the world.
Two weeks later, everyone in Jerusalem
     swarmed the streets on Independence Day.
My friends told me that if a bomb
     was going to explode,
          it would be tonight and here.

The bomb went off in our neighborhood
        at 2:00 in the morning.
My dreams for the rest of the night—
        a Picasso mosaic of fractured gardens,
                light being sucked out of everything.
In Sfat, a Kaballist rabbi read my palm.
        He told me about the future I would avoid
                by leaving.

In a dream, I saw myself—
        a young woman with a scar,
                a field of tiger lilies, an ocean of sky.
A house with a balcony, maybe split timber,
        maybe redwood or white oak
                that grew long ago in a forgotten forest.
White deer ran through the garden—
        their bodies almost made of light.

Two weeks later, in Amsterdam,
        they detained me in the basement of the airport,
                found my suitcase on the tarmac,
walked me to the plane,
        took the magazine I was carrying out of my hand,
                made confetti of my future,
                        and sent me out of the war zone.

We didn't bend with the wind;
        we grew steel in our spines.
Every scar has an edge,
        a canyon, a crater of the moon.
In my house of dreams and split timber,
        I toss sunflower seeds in the garden,
                a shower of tiger lilies, oriental poppies.
I dig in my toes,
        and start to grow.
Life is a koan,
        and the most effective drum
                is the one that makes no sound.

Jeffrey Friedman

Dream in the Garden

Satan came to him in his dream. He handed him a large shiny apple. "Take a bite, and you'll know everything." "I'm not Adam," he answered. "You've got the wrong dream." He threw the apple into the next garden, but as soon as it left his hand another apple appeared, just as red and shiny. "We're in a garden," Satan said. "There's the tree of knowledge, and there's a woman with lovely breasts following you, calling you Adam. I think I have the right dream." "I'm not the only guy," he replied, "with a naked woman with lovely breasts in his dreams. And we're not in a garden. We're in a dream of a garden." "This is my dream," Satan said. Now the woman held the apple, and she was hungry. Though the man ordered her to drop the apple, she ate it vigorously and tossed the core into a bush. "Delicious," she said. "I'll have another."

Alice Friman

Ammunition

for D.H.

My childhood home didn't have
guns from three wars mounted
on the walls as yours did. We had

other weapons. We learned early
how to hone in on the soft parts
without all that metal. We had eye-

darts and below-the-belt ridicule.
We had a stick-it-to-you-you'll-
never-get-rid-of-it shiv in the ribs.

So I'm not impressed by your
Antique Roadshow collection
of flintlocks and Smith & Wessons,

great-grandpa's blunderbuss. Nor
do I envy your born-into-it flags,
rebel yells, and "honorable causes."

My ammo's smeared with older blood,
rue blood, Jew blood, so much blood
the world's sick of hearing about it.

One look at that lady in the harbor
raising a torch to her own platitudes
and we thought we could forget

the malice we'd been taught. Why not?
A new leaf in the book, a new page,
a new start in this America, this

streets-paved-with-gold America
of pushcarts and factory piecework.
Tell me Friend, you with the guns,

what other true-blue Americana
decked your walls? We had Roosevelt.
Franklin Delano. A grinning photo

of the man who was going to save us.
Trouble was, he couldn't save us. Nothing
could save us. Not even the six million

he let slip through his fingers. Six million,
shot, starved, or up the chimney, to add
to our stockpile for future use. Their DNA

roiling down the gutters of Brooklyn,
up the broad avenues of Manhattan,
and across the Hudson to follow us

wherever we went. No, we never had
stashes of guns. We had violins and books.
And if we had to hide or hightail it and run,

we took what we could with us. Sure,
we gave America corned beef on rye,
lox, bagels, and George Gershwin.

Not to mention the Salk vaccine, cheese
danish and Phil Levine. You can't say
we weren't generous. But don't be fooled.

We had weapons. And we could dish it out
with the best of them. Ice-Pick Willie had
nothing on us. He used a gun. We used guilt.

Joanna Fuhrman

I Have a Secret Crush on Everyone in the World

When I say I have a secret crush on everyone
in the world, I mean the earth is a fur-covered
fireball, speeding into the expanding spaces
between paragliding atoms. It means I have
a crush on the way your dangling earlobes
say one thing and your elephant, anxious
hips say another—the way you dial the same
number six times before you build up the nerve
to finish. And yes, it means I am seriously
crushing on your chipped gold nail polish,
the way it signifies a desire to make the world
more beautiful, but also the way it displays
a fuck-you approach to beauty. I was going
to email to say I have a crush on your pre-
apocalyptic recipe poems, but it's 2018
and according to Twitter only old folks
use email. Is there anything more crush-
worthy than a manifesto spelled out in
lightly frosted snickerdoodles, or an essay
floating in a lagoon-shaped swimming pool?
I have a public crush on the number 8 bus,
alfresco Thai brunches and dirty Brooklyn
swans. I love all errors and eras equally.
I have a repressed crush on New Jersey
pollution, the way its oil refineries remind
me I have a nose. To have a crush is to crush
out doubt so thoroughly its green, leathery
skin becomes your own, to taste another's
DNA so purely Januaries dissolve into vats
of frothy vanilla egg creams, spilling into
the cracks of your spine and your loose brain
jelly, into old feet and the cold twitch of your

jaw. To crush is to slide into the neural network
where our wires are made of birdsongs
and magenta-colored loss, is to feel the floor
open and the reverberating metallic shivers after.

Joy Gaines-Friedler

Deportation

I resolve to stop noticing detainees
shuffled into sheriff vans, the unmarked
buildings along the Detroit River.

Resolve—not to feel bereaved,
numbed as a caged 6-year-old.

I'm making my world smaller—

finding Beauty in the faceless
butterfly—all wings and feelers,
conspicuous flight.

Bring holiness into every aspect
of your life—Moses tells us.

I'm making my world smaller—

a little laugh at the wild turkey antics
around the neighbor's deck,

a note on the sidewalk
that reads simply
Yes.

I'm taking a leap around the devastated
islands—it being so *big* an ocean—

trying not to breathe in the fumes & ash,
the acres of fire—I refuse to be consumed
by the wild things seeking escape.

The sonnet they say is the music of love.
I'm listening. I'm listening. *Yes.*

I'm making my world smaller—

eggplant & rosemary, red grapes
or maybe just peanut butter & jelly for dinner.

Vladimir Gandelsman

Stills

A documentary. Death by firing squad.
Last night. I watched.

Someone pushes, let's say, little Dovid
into a pit.

The earth is wet.
Oh look, a hole in his head.

Now there's an apple tree on that hill
in the town of Animalville.

Translated from the Russian by Olga Livshin and Andrew Janco

Robert L. Giron

Like the Mediterranean Tide

Que soy de herencia judía lejana—
the desire to reconnect pulls
and tugs like the Mediterranean tide,
a chant, a scent, a covered portrait
not knowing why: *porque así se hace*
los viernes; yes, on Fridays we cover
the objects, but we're Catholic and
it's not Holy Week.
You say I've a long, distant trail—
muy lejana—quite far
yet the pricks hurt nonetheless.
Nightmares sprung up from "The Nazi Plan,"
nights of anguish and terror
a seven-year-old could not withstand.
What possessed me to fight for the right
to view such a film against my parents'
objection that they did not deny my plea?
—that it made me a pacifist
and one who wept at Kaddish decades later
in "Angels in America" not even
knowing what was said but felt
it deep within?
They say that others see what one
can't yet, years later a simple
test shows the trail—*lejana pero*
fuerte—and so I return to the tide
diluted but vibrant as water itself.

Barbara Goldberg

Furlough

I love to see those tall, lean, muscular men
with their clean-shaven heads and digital

watches toss their kids in the air. And I love
to see them drop, not weightless, but light

as grenades. This is how children learn that fear
can be fun. And fathers, that this too is hand

to hand combat. To cradle or kill—what story
do we tell ourselves to justify. That a *dunam*

of earth is worth dying for? That a child opening
his mouth with an *o* of pleasure overturns

everything? We grow like onions, our heads
buried in dirt. And we die like onions, face

down in a pot of boiling water. Gravity causes
all to fall down, and love, to hold things up.

Janlori Goldman

Yom Kippur

The sunlight didn't break, we are broken,
the word 'broken' is broken —Yehuda Amichai

Today everything hurts, and I'm as close to god as I'll ever come
or want to be. I try to forgive myself, fist knocking at my chest,

a door that forgot how to open. The prayer book's spine
against my palms, I sing loudly to drown out the dandruff

flaked on the suit in the next row, sing as if I believe,
as if the fervor had not been rocked out of me by the cantor

whose polioed leg rubbed into me as we sang together in front
of the high holiday congregation, as if I were still his student

and he could still grip my waist— always his smell of yellow breath
and wear. That was when the old men said girls can never be

rabbis, girls can't stand before the torah. And now in the synagogue,
familiar as the couch leg that catches my pinky toe when I walk past it,

I think of the woman asleep in the window well, blonde wisping
out of a hoodie, sneakers on the sidewalk like slippers by a bed.

No, I'm not hungry, she said. I come to this sanctuary from that chill,
wonder if this is the night I'll open the door. If this is the night.

Ivonne Gordon Carrera Andrade

At Times I See You

among the crowds that emerge from the shadow
at times I see you in the origin
of the room beside the rain.
And I see you
mending with a needle and a light bulb
the memories of war.

I see you in each thread trying to forget your past
like a fish in the air,
I see your eyes reddened by the black thread
in the black stocking scooped from memory
fragile from putting on yourself time and again the same patch.

When I question you
about those times in Charlottenburg
or some other street in Berlin.
You leave with so many unanswered questions.

Like how you escaped from those camps
of unhinged blood.

You fall silent like a Trappist monk
you change the subject.
You go back to the light bulb
to the difficulty of mending an old stocking.

You speak endlessly about the voltage of unknown mailboxes.

I try to gather the threads from the floor
but with your sole you step on my finger
        like a memory of your past.

David Greenstone

The Richest Man Who Ever Lived

I wonder if he had three daughters
with curly blond hair
and attitudes
who grew up too fast right before his eyes
who he tucked into bed each night
one by one
the bedtime ritual growing longer and more complex and later with each
passing year
but always with stories and songs and kisses
and prayers
and then another prayer
that what he had been so blessedly given should not be taken away.
Please. Just please.

The richest man who ever lived
walks the halls of his kingdom each night
after all is quiet
and he knows how small he truly is.
How small it all is. How precarious
how precious
how limited.
He knows and he has always known
and he is terrified.

Roger Greenwald

Why I Am Not an Indian

I am not an Indian because
you've never seen one or you wouldn't ask.
I am not an Indian because
I am a Jew and don't ask
what percentage, when I say Jew
I mean through and through
though few who are Orthodox would say so.
It's true no one knows
where we came from and my mother's mother
with a tan could have looked Mongolian,
could have come from people who millennia before
wandered eastward with their horses and eventually
rode into the cowboy films of my New York childhood
where she, escaped from the pogroms, held a sugar
cube between her teeth
to sweeten her lemony Russian tea.
But if out of principle I insist on census forms
that I am, like all humans,
"of mixed race," still that doesn't mean
I am any more an Indian
than you, so please
look again. Look in.

Marilyn Hacker

Calligraphies II

Self-referential,
a text that explains itself.
Al-Mutanabbi

known by pen, night, desert, sword.
My horse and my notebook think

what I am thinking
through an orgy of cadence.
I loved one woman

whose heart gave out when she read
my letter, that I'd return.

**
He could not return:
price on his head, defector.
His mother, with whom

he talked about books on Skype
through bomb-shattered nights in her

once-tranquil suburb,
was going, not back to the
mountains, not Beirut:

road of the insurrection
in her cells. Could not return.

**
Obsessive return
to the site of departure
or abandonment:

checkpoint south of Reyhanli,
a bar in the rue Charlot—

something changed for good.
She got up and walked away.
A guard waved them through.

And the next day and the next
were going to be different.

**

It is different
waking in the city that
used to be your home.

You are what you are knowing
you are not that anymore,

as old as your friend
when he wrote his late pages
sparring with Bashô

while his sorrel-haired muse fixed
his lunch, pining for cities.

**

The question of lunch,
whether a parenthesis
of conversation

in a cheerful public place
(Tah Marbutah, Hamra Street),

exiles and expats
eating maqdous and kibbeh
in three languages,

or standing near the fridge with
labneh, two verbs, and a spoon.

**

At least two verbs for
departure, five for desire,
come swiftly to mind

from her schoolgirl lexicon.
And all the horses, learned when

she was younger, hoped
to ride away on this new
alphabet, across

deserts of habit and waste
through the six-vocabled dawn.

**

Rainy-fingered dawn
prods the grimy scaffolding
outside the window.

Wet slate roofs, blurry slate sky
swell the list of erasures

you count down, waking.
A sea north of the morning,
a wind from elsewhere –

idea of departure, and
an overstayed welcome.

**

She has overstayed
her transit visa more than
six weeks now. She was

refused a work permit, but
she goes daily to her class,

translates as-Sayyab's
rain song with them to English,
not their first language.

No news from the Ministry
of Labor. War news from home.

**
A long walk home down
the mango-and-sari street,
then the boulevard's

cheap phone cards to Sénégal,
small real estate agents who

upscale old buildings
pricing the immigrants out.
I'd rather live here.

I'd rather live anywhere
than in my worn-out old skin.

**
Under bruise-red skin,
the Pakistani mango's
sweet wet orange flesh,

mix it with labneh in a
blue-purple bowl from Konya—

where your Kurdish friend
said he'd first heard Rumi
in his mother tongue.

All of you sharing treasures
that no one bequeathed to you.

**

He's inherited
another histrionic
refugee. Curses,

silently, his friend, lavish
with others' time and ideas.

Thinks of his uncle's
trek from Lodz to Liverpool
thanks to a letter,

and calls a man who knows a
man in the right ministry.

**

Give the right answer
in the right tone of voice to
the right person who

ate the right thing for lunch and
drank the right dose of caffeine:

you may walk out with
the right papers to claim your
identity card,

your day relentlessly, you
might say, self-referential.

Gili Haimovich

Foreign Weather

I'm in the market
for a foster family
but shopping unsuccessfully.
"The weather is foreign,
not me,
I'm in a good shape
not weathered
just yet"
I say decisively to the
absent mums,
that seem to be sweet as the honey
that we used to lick
in the beginning of the Jewish year
as if this ritual is enough
to sweeten a whole year.
I sweep their shy hands away
with my bitter, not better, hand
"No, no, no, this is the only property I still have left,
my collection of no's."
The truth is
that I'm running out of them faster
then I can afford to admit.
The only real solution
I have come up with,
as of yet,
is hiring a finicky pinkish cat
as my nanny.

Edward Hirsch

A Small Tribe

The legend
of a small tribe
who crossed the steppes
to become Eastern European
eyeglass grinders
with weak eyesight,
horse traders, deserters
from the Russian army,
peddlers, impractical merchants,
men who cried
at the sad stories of women
in tenements, who made
their mothers laugh
over steaming cups of coffee
at the kitchen table,
social democrats
who argued with anarchists
and communists, Zionists
who never travelled to Zion,
failed businessmen
who snuck into Carnegie Hall
to hear Rubinstein playing Chopin
and then stood on a soap box
in Union Square shouting for justice
in the Spanish Civil War,
who loved used bookstores
and the musty back stacks
of old libraries
but started a drug store in Rochester
or sat on his suitcase
waiting for the train
to misfortune
selling shirts on Maxwell Street,
asthmatics, non-assimilators

whose daughters
married developers
who never developed
and scrap metal dealers
looking for an honest advantage,
a gambler who beat the house
and lost everything
three times, a box salesman
who could not contain himself,
a scribbler, my favorite
was a daydreamer
who bought a new hat
every year for Passover
so that he could stand outside
the temple,
which he refused to enter,
though he loved the songs
and wanted to be close
to the prayers.

Jane Hirshfield

My Confession

Immortal soul, I did not believe in you.

Against the age's preference,
I wanted for your markings and history
the markings and history of, say, a small zebra—

slightly implausible, far from unique,
one visible pelt meant to disappear into the crowded many,
one dark stripe alive among the crowded many.

You seemed to want to go on separately.
You seemed to want elsewhere, and more.

I wanted less. One moment to pause
while setting kibble out in a dish for the calico cat
who might or might not
be inside the box when it finally opens.

One goldfinch holding the whole Mesozoic discovery,
hunting for seeds and hungry,
escaping, a few moments longer, the cat also hungry.

This dilemma cannot be solved,
and will be.

My immortal soul, perhaps you went into an *Archelon ischyros*,
swimming with its sea-turtle nose above water,
then diving.

Immortal soul, had you existed,
what more than that cold water could we have wanted?

Paul Hostovsky

Danse Juive

The older I get the more Jewish I look.
I don't feel particularly Jewish
but I look like a Jew. Have you noticed
how some people dance around
the word *Jew?* They don't like to say it.
As if it sounded vaguely pejorative.
As if they only ever heard it used
as a verb. As if it were somehow
offensive to people of the Jewish
persuasion. But I am not persuaded—
I am not of the Jewish persuasion—
but I sure do look like a Jew
with my graying beard and famous nose
and curly hair and glasses. The older I get
the more people are dancing around me.
Everywhere I look these days
the people are dancing. And they're getting
younger and younger the older I get.
They're laughing and singing and dancing
around and around like they're doing the Hora
and I'm this old Jew in the middle
just standing here all alone like a verb
of being. Because I don't know the steps.
And I don't know the time. I don't
even know the words to the song.

W. Luther Jett

Remembrance

This is the suit
I only wear once a year,
if I'm lucky,
on Yom Kippur,
the Day of Remembrance.
My mother's house
sits entirely empty tonight.
Not even a cobweb remains,
and on Monday
the house will be sold
to a man I have not met
but who, I am sure, is kind.
The last time I spoke
with my mother was a long
and difficult phone call,
the threads of it
frayed and straggling.
I was about to ring off
when I remembered
to tell her I wouldn't be calling
the next Friday night.
"It will be Yom Kippur,"
I explained. "Yom Kippur,"
she repeated. Hours later,
my phone rang
and it was not her,
and that was the year
I wasn't so lucky,
and wore this suit
more than once.

Zilka Joseph

Sweet Malida

a mix of water-softened
flattened rice, sugar,
dried fruits and nuts,
was a dish made for
Shabbath or for breaking
fasts. Cooling,
light on the palate, and
to the body and the spirit,
it was welcome in the heat
of day or night. We, like
our Muslim, Christian and Hindu
neighbors and friends,
had many foods in common,
and we often celebrated together
their festivals or ours. I relished
particularly fresh coconut,
the regional staple, its milk
or its flesh added to almost
every dish. But this was to me
the best way to eat it,
finely grated
by my mother's hands,
left unsweetened
and sprinkled haphazardly
on the malida, juicy threads
with a fleck of stubborn
brown kernel here and there
that sometimes crunched
in your teeth like sand,
and you winced and swallowed it,
knowing that there was no
simpler or purer
or truer form than that.

Marilyn Kallet

Removed

—March 19, 2012

At the Franciscan friary all the news is apple blossoms,
white opposum, ghosts in the historic barn.

I'm too removed, won't be reminded
of anti-Semitism, fresh murders in Belle France.

A French-Algerian gunned down a paratrooper,
three French soldiers, then a teacher and three children

at Ozar Hatorah, their Jewish elementary school.
Toulouse lies an hour from our workshop in Auvillar,

farther from this friary in rural Indiana.
Bullets don't ricochet

overseas. The anti-Semitism that killed keeps killing. I'm
removed. Here the news is Eastern Bluebirds.

I don't hear shooting, jihadists.
Won't write about Paris gendarmes, cheered

by the Gestapo. The *rafles*—roundups,
not winning tickets. July, 1942.

Drancy. 2012, the French come to terms
with cardboard memorials,

and a lone railway car.
The plaza hosts a circus and drug deals.

Septfonds.
Auschwitz.

What I do know.

Ilya Kaminsky

Dancing in Odessa

We lived north of the future, days opened
letters with a child's signature,

a raspberry, a page of sky.
My grandmother threw tomatoes
from her balcony, she pulled imagination like a blanket
over my head. I painted
my mother's face. She understood
loneliness, hid the dead in the earth like partisans.

The night undressed us (I counted
its pulse) my mother danced, she filled the past
with peaches, casseroles. At this, my doctor laughed, his granddaughter

touched my eyelid—I kissed
the back of her knee. The city trembled,
a ghost-ship setting sail.
And my classmate invented twenty names for Jew.
He was an angel, he had no name,
we wrestled, yes. My grandfathers fought

the German tanks on tractors, I kept a suitcase full
of Brodsky's poems. The city trembled,
a ghost-ship setting sail.
At night, I woke to whisper: yes, we lived.
We lived, yes, don't say it was a dream.

At the local factory, my father
took a handful of snow, put it in my mouth.
The sun began a routine narration,
whitening their bodies: mother, father dancing, moving
as the darkness spoke behind them.
It was April.

The sun washed the balconies, April.
I retell the story the light etches
into my hand: *Little book, go to the city without me.*

Jen Karetnick

In Poverty of Climate, People of Other Are Known as Lichens

Dandruff on the scalp of the earth,
we layer between desert sand,
slag heap and Arctic tundra where

nothing else roots, not even a mirage
of a river that parts to make way
or the aurora borealis, festering in hues

too toxic to be natural. No matter
what our books say, only hate opens
for passage, only fear commands.

There is no manna. If it falls,
it's from a heaven we no longer
believe in anyway. A test-tube

ecosystem reproducing our same
selves, we live on smog and cement
to grow forward a millimeter at a time.

We do no harm but are well
aware that too many of us together
will be seen as a sign of sickness.

We are always ready for the breaking
of the bough, the knives that scrape
us loose for feeding to the fire,

the salutes and jackboots that kick us
out to colonize yet another crust of shell
or fractured gravestone kind of place.

We were among the first to arrive
on this fresh rock; our genes date
the cooling. But those who insist on

viewing us as unwanted guests
who showed up at the party too early,
carrying our coats and wine for each other,

must also know that we will always
be the last to leave, outstaying even
the most barren, inhospitable host.

Gennady Katsov

An Invective

Do not build cities where cemeteries once stood:
In their infrastructures, their pipes and foundations,
Horror still grows that oozes out of the corpses,
And the storehouse of faith and infidelity clogs up.

Do not build cities over places of execution,
Nor over sanctuaries, and never over a battlefield,
For no desire will be so fulfilled, for what's to come,
Its outcome will be made only more atrocious.

Nor should cities be established in times of confusion
Or during periods of crisis, or havoc, or epidemic:
They will emerge like phantoms out of nightmares
In the form of bats that come to one in bad dreams.

And this someone who will eventually awaken among
Necropoli, places of execution, barracks, Place d'Armes,
That are everywhere and always, deeded to the future,
Will not stumble over streets paved with grave stones.

Translated from the Russian by Alex Cigale

Judith J. Katz

Mit'ti'a' eech

for Yisrael Levitz

There is a Hebrew word
for when old graffiti
is covered with new graffiti
without first removing
what was there.

The process of painting
a new layer without
first removing the previous
layer.

Archaeological
like an aging mind
leaving ghosts
of languages, images.

A collage over a collage
of memories ever there
a lifetime of darkness
and light.

The beginning of the desire
to become.
The fear that
stops us in our tracks.

Tell me your ancient graffiti
and I will tell you mine
and in the telling
we will begin anew.

Julia Knobloch

Saint Lawrence River from the Plane

for Leonard Cohen

The great river I wanted to see since I was twelve
streams below me to the north-east.

Thin ice floes swirl around the islands, past
silent reed grass and stiff poplars, the clock tower

on the pier. This is the birthplace of your poetry,
where tea and oranges touched your mind.

You taught me to lean out for love,
I lean against the window.

Along the skyline, translucent smoke floats
over black-lit copper, charcoal, bronze, and white—

the only green, for one moment,
the bridge and lady of the harbor. And then

the holy mountain where you are, frozen earth.

Nina Kossman

[Like lambs]

Like lambs, they were led to slaughter,
without being told anything,
but a god peered out of the ditch,
into which the corpses rolled,
as he peered through the cracks
of barracks and crematoria,
which were built by people
on the orders of other people;
poor god, he was not consulted
when they were killing millions,
and now they say there is no god
since he allowed so many to be killed.
And that god was one of those lambs,
who they led to slaughter;
he was one of those black-eyed boys,
a mother with an infant at her breast,
an old woman limping up to the ditch's edge,
nobody knew about this —
neither those who gave the order to shoot
mother and child — as one
to economize on bullets,
nor those who saw and forgot,
so nothing could trouble their sleep.
And afterwards the earth breathed,
as if the corpses were moving,
and one got up, not quite dead,
and began to walk the forest path,
which no one else had walked,
slept in bushes (moss was as soft as a bed)
ate berries for dinner,
his eyes, grown large with hunger,
gazed on hares and squirrels,
while wolves and other beasts
let him be, they knew better than to eat a god;

and so he survived two years,
and when he came out of the forest,
villagers surrounded him, pointing at him, pointing,
look, a walking corpse
(that god was mangy like Mowgli),
saying, go away, away from here,
nothing's left for you here anymore.
So he went away and lived into his old age
in rooms close by the sea,
in a town called Bat Yam,
(better than *yama*, the god joked),
and when he died
nothing of him remained
except an old notebook,
and in it two words:
"I survived."

That page was torn out,
placed in a museum,
and that's all I know about that god.

Translated from the Russian by Mary Jane White

Helene Seltzer Krauthamer

Soul Food

Perhaps the universe began
with a sprinkling of yeast,
stardust,
water,
time and space
for the mix to expand and contract
in the warmth of a billion suns
pounding and kneading
the cosmic bagel.

Bruce Lader

A Proposal

Far be it from me, a low-wage earner,
to advise anyone on fiscal affairs.
Even so, a little ordinary savvy
tells me that You, being the Omnipotent,
might have mercy, transfer about a trillion
out of the lopsided military budget
and accounts of the loaded top percent,
distribute the funds in a more
altruistic and equitable manner

to refugees and others subsisting on less
than a daily dollar, many starving,
dying of diseases. Why not prioritize?
Yes they do what's possible
to further themselves. No I don't believe
the deity that billions assume
set time in motion, can overschedule.

Surely You, The Inventor of every
sound, sense, event, and deed,
always listening with empathy,
conceiver of electromagnetic fields
that bind the molecules of everything,
You hear their troubled voices,
though deafening terrorists
try to drown them out.

I know the embryonic stage
of my plan to aid the destitute
sounds risky. Nevertheless, I would not
attempt to bargain a nebulous project
were I not convinced the venture can
coalesce into a marketable system with
a touch from You of the munificent
magic life-force they desperately need.

As a good-faith gesture, upon
the reply of your Benevolent Spirit,
I will sign a legal document giving You
full ownership. I won't get a cent.

Joy Ladin

A Modest Proposal

Let's not kill or die today.
Let's make angels out of yarn, men of snow, mashed potato animals
that smile as we spoon
their eyes of melted butter.

Instead of killing ourselves or one another,
let's neatly stack anxiety's sweaters
and scratch our itchy trigger fingers
by whittling turtles for our mothers,

or pretending to understand Heidegger,
or imagining the sexual embrace
through which time and space
first conceived of matter.

If we still aren't over killing and dying,
we can search the stacks for library books
that haven't circulated in generations
and savor the mold

that spores their spines
the way wine snobs savor the nose
of vintage wines bottled
between wars to end all wars.

Look, we've played all day
and haven't spilled a drop of blood
apart from the occasional paper cut.
In an hour or two, when it's very dark,

let's make up stories out of stars,
and fill them with all the killing and dying

we didn't do today, except in our imaginations.
Let's pull our comforters over our heads

and sing ourselves to sleep
like good little civilizations.

David K. Leff

Koufax

Homers are dandy, but who needs them with Sandy.
      —a ditty from childhood

Born on opening day at Ebbets Field
in the only year his long suffering hometown Dodgers
took the subway Series from baseball's fence-
busting aristocrats, I was my father's good luck charm.

At age eight I hurried home from school to see
the Series opener on a jittery twelve-inch black-and-white
screen, watching Koufax stretch in mighty muscular
arcs that fooled a record fifteen Bronx Bombers

looking or swinging. Goliaths Kubek, Maris, Pepitone,
Mantle, and Tresh were no match, and when pinch
hitter Harry Bright whiffed for the final out, I leapt
from the couch like I'd thrown the last pitch. At Shea

Stadium two years later in '65, full with a hot dog
and Coke, I sat awestruck as he mowed down Met
after Met, staring at batters with calm ferocity,
the ball seeming to disappear as it approached the plate

but for a gunshot pop into the catcher's mitt.
Besting the great Spahn in a twelve-strikeout-one-
hitter on the greenest grass I'd ever seen, he had a dancer's
fluid grace, a boxer's animal power. One leg

anchored to the ground, the other kicked so far skyward
it seemed he might fly from the mound
while reaching back for a fastball that could set
the air afire, or a razor curve that broke in defiance

of physics. First day of the Series, I chanted
the ancient dirges for justice, mercy, and atonement

knowing Sandy would utter the same sacred words.
More than a ballplayer, the Rabbi explained,

a *mentsch* who played in pain for his team, who knew
an authority higher than the game I worshiped.
Still, to the Torah's rhythmic melody I snuck out
to a classroom where men and boys in *kippot*

davened to the play-by-play on a tiny television.
In tears the next year when Koufax quit the mound
at the apex of skill, little did I know that he grew
increasingly vulnerable as he became unhittable,

his pitching arm crippled with arthritis, only kept
pliable in endless baths of heat and ice. At thirty,
he left behind money and cheering crowds, never to feed
on the carcass of his fame like those perennial

ghosts of greatness signing balls and programs at bush
league games and sports shows, selling coffee
makers or undershorts, trading on their faded youth
as pitchmen for casinos and mortgage lenders.

A kid watching butterflies in right field exile, I endured
taunts owing to the Koufax within. Today his photo
smiles forever with spring training hope among my family
portraits, for reasons not much to do with baseball.

Merrill Leffler

What I Want of It

I want it to graze like gazelles and soar with the aplomb of hawks.

I want it to rise like a palace out of syllables of breath.

I want it to open locked gates with obscure incantations.

I want it to kick down locked doors and lead into meadows of starlight.

I want it to light up the night with meteors of radiance and desire.

I want it to inflame the coldness of my heart and set passion on fire.

I want it to waken the mountain gods and startle the dead from boredom.

I want it to revive my ancestors and ask for their blessings.

I want it to guide me through deserts year after year and lead me to water
and wild fruit.

I want it to open my eyes and reveal angels ascending and descending in my
own backyard.

David Lehman

Sabbath Feast (excerpt from "Yeshiva Boys")

How beautiful to me are the red fire-escapes of my youth.

How goodly to me are the tents of morning housing the tenants of dry seasons in books read and reread until mastered in old age by tigers who crouch at the edge of the jungle ready to pounce.

How happy the wife who prepares the Sabbath feast.

How happy the son who knows by heart the benediction following the meal.

How happy the daughters who recite the verses of the Bible for their father's pleasure. This week Jacob wrestles the angel of god to a standstill.

How purple the stain of the wine on the white tablecloth, how sweet the ruby wine, how cool the taste on the lips and tongue, how full of zest the grape as it bursts into life in the mouth.

How savory with salt the yellow bread, broken into pieces and blessed, and eaten standing up.

How sweet to the man are the days of his youth. How surprised he would be, could he hear his own voice clamoring for attention at the dinner table with his parents and sisters and perhaps an uncle and aunt on a Friday night in 1961.

Jeffrey Levine

Aymat Zibur

—among Orthodox Jews, fear of public prayer

One morning I find her walking upright.
I say, you're walking upright!
What do you mean, she asks.
I mean, that you're not bent over,
how you've been for years, like Odysseus
when he enters the Great Hall with arrows
up his sleeve, bent more and more, nearly doubled over.
She says, again with the Odysseus.
She says, upright?
Yes, you're standing totally straight!

There are prayers we don't even bother praying.
How could this happen, I ask her.
How could what happen?
That you're standing straight, unbent, tall!
I'm amazed! Amazed at what? she asks.
I think of what Athena does for Odysseus,
Taller, younger, stronger, what she does for Penelope.
Taller, more commanding, and like Prince Telemachus,
Zeus up there has robbed me of my wits, and no gods sing.

The head nurse says she's unsurprised.
I'm not surprised, she says, because, she says,
this morning I told her to stand up straight. And me,
how to know which sacrifice is right for the new gods.
Afraid to pray the Lord my soul to keep
or take, this divine ailment, this sacred madness,
like a demon barely under control.

Would you bring fire, you will agree
to have your liver eaten every night,
done in time for the early news.
What is the penalty for prayer? Oh,

not to be, what, ninety-five.
How old was Prometheus, fatally public
with his stolen fire? How old Moses
with his cancelled visa?

I take her out to lunch at The Hellenic,
she with her walker, still standing tall,
I'm thinking, my God, this is a miracle,
I should thank God right here, right now,
the *bracha* for standing tall, and me with my fear

of prayer in my shoes, and everywhere people davening
into their spanikopita, oceans of hot avgolemeno soup,
all eyes averted from our glacial progress, everyone pained,
everyone thinking, I will never be so old or so slow,
the walker propped out of the sight of the Lord against a wall,
her hands the hands of the suffering, tortured, starfish fingers,
blacks and blues, claw, straight-backed to the table.

How can this be? What prayers have you not invented?
Don't be silly, she says. At my age, things do and undo.
And anyway, next morning, again her back is bowed,
worse than ever, like she's an extra in a horror film.

There is a time for prayer, but there is no prayer like silence.
Best not to steal the soul of the unknown, nor
for that matter, of the known. Something happens,
something un-happens.

Matthew Lippman

Keeping Kosher

Remember your car in Maryland
when it was followed
by another car wrapped in Reichstag red
we were talking about the Beastie Boys
you said hold on
I said what
you said look behind
it was a summer night
we had eaten a dungeon of Dungeness crabs
drank a barrel of beer
I used a steak knife on butter
we buried it in the backyard
you said it will take 30 days
we won't tell my mother
I didn't know
I don't know still
you pumped the gas pedal
the brake
driving east into the darkness
the sun slipping between suburbia and swastika
there was one stitched into the other driver's face
you saw it
did you see it
I did
you did one of those Steve McQueen movie moves
pulled into a driveway
turned off the headlights
like we had been parked there all afternoon
they drove right past
I never understood till then
how close you can get to death in suburbia
nothing changes
today an 18 year old named Matthew Lipp from your hometown
got busted for spray painting the n word wrapped inside a swastika

curled inside the belly of a pig
on a wall outside the gym
that's how close the hate is,
it's one syllable away,
the *man* after *lipp*
missing

Olga Livshin

Eating a Persimmon, 1954

At four years old, in her grandpa's lap,
sun-warmed inside an Odessa courtyard,
my mother tests out a persimmon.

She has never met such weird fruit:
sweet jellyfish creepy-crawling.
Nu, es, little *meydeleh,* eat,

her grandpa glows at her, a Jewish wizard
visiting from a collective farm.
His beard smells like cow poop.

In quiet Russian, she asks: *Grandpa,
do people actually like per-sim-mons?*
Oh, *mansy!* Silly stories!—he brushes her off.

*Is this why I walked all over the Privoz Market
for one perfect piece of fruit I could afford—
just for you? Have some good* seylch *and eat.*

My mother sighs and tries to swallow the globe,
which spins sixty quick times around the sun,
finding her with her grandson and me,

all of us considering a bowl of conical,
identical supermarket Hachiyas, freckled
by California, where she lives these days.

And this story she tells us. And Adam,
with his *nyet, thanks but no thanks, Grandma,
for that fruit.* And my mom, who decides

to reveal, then, the DNA of our family's
eating: a pogrom, she says, chewed up
an uncle as he ran to shelter;

the world chomped on a branch
of our family deer-like, just needing to eat,
just minding its own business,

for instance, a six-year-old boy—
had he not died, he'd be an older brother
to my mother. She was not born yet,

the first child to sprout in that great
mishpooha after the war. *They all gave me treats,*
she smiles sadly: *Going a bit hungry themselves.*

I ask what a treat was back then.
A handful of sugar? How tenuously godlike,
I think to myself, her grandfather

must have felt about that persimmon,
thinking he was giving my mother
the chance to be—just this once—

the eater. How, instead, he gave her
an order, force-feeding the love of forced
feeding, the unsubtle art of forcing

that I spoon-feed to Adam, with a dash
of Russian, which passes for some Vitamin R—
supposed to make a child feel Rooted.

How there is still another interpretation
for that persimmon: my great-grandfather
wanted his only grandkid to know pleasure.

To dive into an unexplored space:
neither the unwatered earth,
nor trauma's infinite hug,

but softness.

Dennis Maloney

Excerpt from "Border Crossings"

3

In the capitals and squares of Europe
people gather to support the Falun Gong, refugees
fleeing Syria, and victims of the genocide in Armenia.
Under the Brandenburg gate they celebrate the
World Cup win. I hear the rare chant of hare krishna,
an almost extinct species in America.

In the dark shadows the nights of broken glass
reemerge, as the persecuted are confused
with the persecutors; and marches and rallies
against all that is foreign stream into the night.

Irina Mashinski

Russia

In that land, where it's hard to say "Jew,"
the wind breaks open its tightly-sealed doors,
                    a low sky runs above my head—
and those who wait for me are just leaves, trunks.
The city's sharp elbows—corners—
                    are grey at the bottom—and then suddenly blue.

And beyond the city limits, after rain,
the jellied-clay gleams as a hundred watt bulb
                    like nowhere else.

There many stand in harness and go nowhere.
Outside—there the water stands.
                    There no one commands the waters: "Part."

There men are hard pressed and martins blessed,
there I hardly see myself—I tell you—
                    (and in this there is nothing, nothing)—

there, until dawn—no one throws back the bolt.
There it's still five, still six o'clock.
                    You sleep—I stay awake.

As along the rail-bed a milk of fog spills
down—shallowly, and then suddenly deep:
                    into it, like people, the far lights move,

there the forest stands with its eyes sealed shut,
there you are free to stand before it, or fall to your knees,
                    free to light a candle, free to burn yourself out.

Translated from the Russian by Mary Jane White

Jed Myers

Jewish Cemetery Night

Those headstones at Mount Carmel, each
must weigh more than a man, and taken
a couple of men apiece to bring down,
one then the next, nearly a hundred,
into the night. This was a team,
I imagine—together they pressed
their shoulders and chests and cheeks
and palms in uncanny brief intimacies
into the names of women and men
who walked the Northeast Philly streets
before these raiders were born. I see
the impression of some part of *loving
father* remain for minutes embossed
in the pad of flesh under a thumb. Another's
brow is stamped with the Hebrew letter
aleph that stands for the first of the Ten
Commandments. I hear the men grunt
in unison on the heave after *three*.

And the gratification, the bonding
these guys, I'm sure they're young, must be
able to feel, with what they've achieved—
what lives have they been leading? Is this
as close to a shared heatedly held
meaning as they can get, faceless
amalgam of the dead under their feet
and available to be blamed? The hugs
these topplers must've exchanged, shined
by their sweat in the moonlight. What lives
led to this? That it was just common
hate could uplift them? Don't they drink
their pints after work in the tavern, cheer
and curse the game over the bar? Doesn't it

keep their hides secure round their hearts
and their eyes off each other? I think
it's that secret aloneness does it, down
in the dark, dark as the dirt.

Yvette Neisser

The Whole Imperfect Lot of Us

—Yom Kippur, 2010

You must change your life,
say the rabbis of old.
Shine a mirror inside yourselves,
examine your flaws.
Scrub the soul clean.

As we sit in silence,
one boy cannot control his voice.
Now and then he lets out a howl,
shaking us out of contemplation.

Bless him for digging deep.

Bless us all, the whole imperfect lot of us—
the ones with hair combed neatly
        and those with unruly hair
the ones who stand still in prayer
        and those who shuffle from foot to foot
the ones who pray aloud
        and those who pray silently
the ones who barely mutter the words
        and those who simply hum the tune
the ones with eyes fixed on the prayer book
        and those whose eyes wander the room.

Bless the one whose voice awakens us
        and those who look away.

Leslie B. Neustadt

Migration at Rosh Hashanah

My Judaism slips away,
stutters into silence.
      Hebrew's honeyed letters
            no longer sweeten the blackboard.
Vowels offer no redemption
in the wasteland of Hebrew consonants.
      My roots so overgrown,
            they merge into the nothingness
                  where faded memories live.
I'm often drawn to circles
where I'm the only Jew.
Yet Judaism unlocks a roadblock
      to Shana Leah, my beloved self.
No *l'dor v'dor* in my family,
I find myself celebrating
      the arrival of 5779 with a flock of swifts
            who alight in Portland en route to Mexico.
Their migration part of the great mystery,
an inner knowing woven with feathered genes.
      The swifts circle the stars, then slumber
in a chimney at my grandson's elementary school.
Visiting from Upstate New York,
I find Congregation Havurah Shalom
      and for a few hours, I return to my flock,
            breathe in the familiar chants and weep.
The same prayers and lamentations
heard in temples around the globe.
      My childhood devotions return to me.
            I wrap myself in a *tallit*, cover my head in white,
                  claim my birthright to have an *Aliyah* to bless the Torah.
I open the door to the stranger who is myself.
      I want to stay until the last drop of honeyed prayer.

Rachel Neve-Midbar

What the Light Reveals

—Har Hazaytim, Jerusalem

Marble boxes cover this hill, graves
crumbled and aged, the color of teeth,
row after row facing east; buried

here are you who will rise
first, call back to the others, enter
the world of endless life. Your names

echo through generations,
like the lamplighter who walks,
torch in hand, moves

slowly from one grave to the next,
sending a glow into the darkening
night. Or perhaps just a match

set to a wick of pure olive oil,
the light clean and clear
as a summer day, sunlight

so bright we hide our eyes,
and fruit that ripens only
in the long heat of the summer sun,

fruit whose names define us:
Tamar, Te'ena, Rimon, Zayit,
whose shade shields us, whose

pips and stems compost back into the soil
on this eastern side of the hill,
where lights come on slowly with the dusk—

East Jerusalem with its cacophony of cars
and marquees, the green lights
of minarets kindled

one after the other, dotting the way
far into the folds of the desert.
Muezzins who call out,

one leading to the next—
voices, mournful, undulating—pleas
so like the shofar cries

that drift up these stone stairs, call us
back to where we come from— this umbilicus
that whispers a soul to a soul. Your names:

Keila, Pessel, Shaindela, Ruchel: you,
who loved to knead the dough: you,
who danced the hem

of her wedding dress to pieces: you,
who died in the Grodno Ghetto,
giving birth on a dirty floor,

and though we never knew your stories
our souls still told the truth, the death
was not easy. This is why we can't sleep.

And the wind that once
blew cold in Belarus, now hot
and dry over this eastern hill.

No more lamplighters:
we are Nava, Odelyia, Yael,
and electricity now scrambles

the light between the words,
whispers rise like mist, a simple
wish that wherever we are

we can hearken back to the sweet pink
of a western sky, the last kiss of daylight
as traffic fades, the stars unveil

themselves, the muezzins now quiet. Wherever
you are, tell us why we need any answers,
tell us what any light will reveal.

Lesléa Newman

13 Ways of Looking at 9/11

I.
First thought:
This is not good
for the Jews.
Second thought:
This is not good
for the lesbians.
Third thought:
this is not good
for me.

II.
Even now—especially now
the body has its demands:
the belly cries to be fed.
But food can't push past
the lump of tears
stuck in my throat
too terrified
to spill from my eyes

III.
The cats, usually so aloof
except at feeding time
stay close
unaware, yet knowing
something heavy
soft and purring
is needed on my lap

IV.
Born in Brooklyn
raised on Long Island,
I moved to Manhattan

to seek fame and fortune
then fled the city twenty years ago.
Still, in my heart I am a New Yorker
so people call,
wanting to connect
wanting it to be their tragedy, too.
"Did you lose anyone?"
they ask, almost hopeful.
I am almost sorry to disappoint them.

V.
The nation is on high alert.
I stock canned goods in the basement,
stash two hundred dollars
under my mattress
thinking, *this and a token
will get me a ride on the subway.*
Then I remember
where I live
there is no subway

VI.
The search dogs get depressed;
there are so few bodies to be found.
One team stages a mock recovery
to boost their dogs' morale.
A burly firefighter
puts down his gear,
lies down in the rubble
and like a dog, plays dead.
Soon the search dogs start to bark
and wag their tails
and lick his face.
Soon the firefighter rises from the ashes
and slowly walks away

VII.
Bags and bags of body parts:
finger, ankle, elbow.
I remember lying in bed with you
looking at our feet sticking up

from under the blankets,
yours so brown and slender,
a perfect size six with ballerina arches;
mine so pale and squat and flat.
We joked about knowing each other in a crowd
solely by our feet.
Now I try to wrap my mind
around the unimaginable:
a knock at the door,
I open it to a stranger
who hands me your right foot
and I am grateful even for that.

VIII.
It doesn't take long
for the newspapers
to quote letters
blaming Israel and the Jews.
It doesn't take long
for the newspapers
to quote Jerry Falwell
blaming the feminists and the gays.
It doesn't take long
for me to stop reading
the newspapers.

IX.
In my little town
at my little grocery store
a cashier refuses to check out
a woman he calls a "turban head,"
a woman I call a cancer survivor.

X.
It is the longest we have gone
in thirteen years
without making love.
Finally I let you touch me
though I feel I might shatter
like glass. Those who died
will never enjoy

this gift again.
How dare I waste it?

XI.
A blank notebook page
an empty computer screen,
what is the point of writing anything?
Then an unbidden email from a fan:
"Thank you for bringing so much
beauty into my heart and the world."
Tears tumble from my eyes.

XII.
I dream a child stands
on the twin towers
of her sturdy legs
before she disappears
and I am running
across the Brooklyn Bridge,
naked and burning,
my skin falling away
like the Vietnamese girl
in that famous photo.
Everyone I ask for help
asks me, "Are you an Arab
or a Jew?" I tell them,
"I am a human being"
and everyone who hears my answer
vanishes like smoke

XIII.
On Rosh Hashanah
there is a discussion group at the synagogue.
Our leader says when she first heard,
she was so angry she wanted to kill
somebody—anybody—and everybody
she spoke with felt the same way.
"Is there anyone here
who isn't furious?" she asks.
I look around the circle,
then slowly raise my hand
like a white flag of surrender.

Jean Nordhaus

Interfaith

We made our pact. We would celebrate
all holidays, though we believed in none—
the more the merrier: Santa Claus and
Chanukah gelt, Easter eggs and matzoh balls,
bonfires at the Pueblo on Christmas eve as the men
in their blankets, the guards in their uniforms
lifted the solemn virgin in her painted Sukkot
to their shoulders and danced her, precarious,
around the plaza, guns going off, the fires
crackling, bullet casings in the sand.
It was all, all a wonder, a glorious jumble
of old and new, a panoply, a shopping spree.
Why limit ourselves to one God, one tribe,
when we could have it all? We believed in *life*.
In celebration—and kept a bottle of champagne
tucked on its side in the fridge, in case.
Now that you're gone, and I'm alone
I've joined the synagogue of skeptics,
where I belong, where I'm at last at home.

Joshua Sassoon Orol

Minyan מנין

When a man is in mourning
nine others are needed
before he can say out loud
that god is good.

It is forbidden for a man
to hold a blade
even a safety razor
against his own neck.

It is expected that he will pray
with his hair covered
by both kippah and shawl.

I get the call
in front of the full-length mirror—
Hey man we need a tenth

trap the phone against my shoulder
and fondle the gelled breasts
filling out my borrowed bra
nibble at my dark lipstick
finger the high slit
on my calfskin skirt.

One more grieving man.
Will I not let him weep?

Leonard Orr

Cemetery Therapy

In my youth, my mother took me along
for visits to the long-dead relatives.
We were always formally dressed for
these excursions; I wore ties and suits,
black, brown, or blue, smaller versions
of the suits my father wore every day
when he went to his dental office.
My mother wore colorful dresses and
matching high heels and other accessories.
If asked, she could say in what recent
issue of Vogue or other thick, glossy,
heavily perfumed magazine, she had
first seen those pieces that made up
the ensemble for today's outing. Her
few years modeling coats in fashion shows
and newspaper ads gave her grounding
and wisdom. If she saw a camera
in the vicinity, she snapped into
what we knew as "the pose,"
with brilliant smile and bright red hair.
Whenever we went to her mother's grave
she told me the same stories (her mother
died of tsurris) and then updated her mother
on what was going on with all of relatives,
with their illnesses and celebrations, with
bad clothing or flawed in-laws and children.
Then she would weep while I handed her
tissues from a new box we brought along
for just that moment. It was the second
weeping. The cemetery days began with
an anguished, teary singing along to
Connie Francis' song "Mama." After,
by the time we were seated at the counter
of The Hamburger Train, her makeup
was perfect, tranquility was restored.

Jacqueline Osherow

A Meise of Rabbi Simkha's Zayde

My rabbi friend's *zayde,*
Meir Chaim, of blessed memory,
sold candy from a pushcart
in nineteen twenties? thirties? Montreal
(or, rather, *meant* to sell;
he had a soft heart
and the children in his neighborhood were poor).
He bore, on his cheek, an enormous scar
where a passing Cossack's sword
had hacked off his God-fearing beard
and inadvertently
saved his life, since, consequently,

Chaim Meir fled his home
and thereby missed his shtetl's conflagration —
a bit like my great uncle, who, thanks to Stalin,
was safe in the gulag
when the *einzatzgruppen* came.
(Their procedure: to make the able-bodied dig

an enormous ditch, then shoot them into it,
on top of them, less brawny family members.)
My friend, the rabbi, vividly remembers
his mild-mannered *zayde*, meek, demure,
watching boxing matches late into the night:
to see one goy hit another, it gives me pleasure.

To me, it's a deadly funny story;
blame my acrid Ashkenazic sense of humor,
nursed on victimhood, catastrophe, lament.
Not that I, myself, have earned its vantage point,
my life amazingly unscathed by history
except as a terrifying rumor.

(Thus far, that is; let's not goad
an already restless evil eye.) Still, for me, a joke
is tactic, analgesic, parable:
Moishe and Yankl before a firing squad:
how, Moishe, for his last request, asks to smoke
and Yankel begs him *Moishe, don't make trouble.*

This, too, I find eternally hilarious
but who's now left to get the punch line?
Who's standing before a firing squad?
and who — God
help us — now holds the gun?

Alicia Ostriker

The Laptop Also Is Dying

Born in the last decade of the last,
I mean previous, century,

it took me awhile to recognize
that she was ready to die.

First she became unable to remember where
things were, then every gesture and motion slowed

and sometimes halted and had to be restarted
while a strange rainbow wheel endlessly whirled on the screen

like something ecstatic bursting out of Ezekiel
that might be wordless laughter or a scream.

The long interval between my thought and her response
inevitably disturbed me. I understood

she meant this as a message
about life, about the world

in which everything winds down
and we cannot help grieving,

but what a couple, what a *pair* we were,
brimming with energy back then we flew

intermingled and interchanged our ghosts
our ancestors like shadows while we flew

and *she* was also a *he* or no gender at all, like a cloud, like dust,
back then, back then when I had something to say

a new song for the God I don't believe in
an argument for the God I wanted to love.

Alan Michael Parker

Yehuda Amichai Probably Knows My Lover's Name

Yehuda Amichai is funnier than I am, and sexier
because he's smarter. He's never
afraid to be wrong, or to balance
the Spoon of Destiny on his nose, having licked
the Spoon of Destiny first. He never says
that my poems are a party trick.

He's the man behind the counter who
short-changes you so that you return.
He's the man with the smile like heat lightning

over the Mississippi on a Tuesday evening
from the window of a plane, Seat 14A
and I'm in 14B. Now that's a smile.

He's the man whose body matters
less for its shape than its style.
Yehuda Amichai, I hate your great poems

today as I fly away from my love,
from home to some Ramada Inn
that's a Museum of YesterWoe, the bed linens

turned down in a frown on the sixth floor of Hell
where the mirror and the TV and the locked door
that won't open onto the balcony

renounce me. The phone's infected.
The sunset's on Auto. The staff is nice.
The Carpet of Forgiveness

takes care of every spill.
Yehuda Amichai's great poems lie
open on the spongy bedspread

while ESPN counts down the past
in a hotel room with one other book,
a hotel room with wars on thirty channels.

Linda Pastan

Kristallnacht

was the word I heard
my parents whisper behind
closed doors. And I pictured
the world under a sudden
enchantment of ice, each tree limb
braceleted in crystal, each lamppost,
each windshield glazed
and electrically gleaming,
the very air wincing with light.
And the only sound would be
a myriad tinkling,
as of a thousand thousand
miniature wind chimes.
The treacherous beauty of words.
Crystal night: the stars themselves
blazing and frozen in place.

Marge Piercy

Shalom in my mouth like a kumquat bitter then sweet

about peace, shalom, shalom
when we've never known it?

Our land in Eretz Israel, always
contested, still is. Penned
into ghettoes crowded as factory

animals in their stalls barely
wide enough to stand. Books
burnt. Then us. Auto de fe—

whose faith was tested? Even
when we thrust roots deep,
into nations, hatred seeks us.

Peace is that promise we dream—
the city on the hill shining golden
but maybe that's just the sun

setting that gilds it. Shalom
is hope, hope that breathes
through all our year's prayers.

Making peace is the only way
to know it. I wrap that hope
around me like a tallit.

Susan Rich

Pregnant with the Dead

I am a woman swollen with the history of my dead,
great aunts and second cousins murdered

in the old country—bloated with fragments of survivors

who hid months in garbage cans, others in partisan forests;
I'm their bandaged daughters gauzed from toe to forehead

to keep safe from search patrols, from their first rapes.

Yes, I am a body awash in stories of noodle kugel, borscht—
watch the heavy arms of the women waving like sails

as they knead challah each Friday morning,

can't conceive of a few hours free.
What can I do with the women who occupy my vertebrae,

take over my hips and tongue?

They say *coconut bars, mundel bread, hamantaschen.*
They say *that's your problem* as they stride

into my kitchen, toss out the nonfat yogurt, the tofu treats.

It is a rumba of before and after.
And of course, many *volk* murdered—

abducted our young girls, butchered our sons.

And now, my dead tell me, it's time to enjoy
a brioche—a week in *the Disneyland*.

Don't my dead deserve to mist their skin with *Shalimar*

at the airport perfume cathedrals?
Enough time spent on nightmares!

Instead let us hike up the heat, make selfies.

And later, when it quiets on the hotel balcony,
we vanish like light vessels, almost escaped out to sea.

Kim Roberts

Prophecy

The Sword of Damocles hovers
over the sliced pastrami,
the lox glistens with nervous sweat,

the dill trembles and hides among the pickles
and trepidation makes the bagels
curl inward.

I am the Cassandra of the Delicatessen
and you will not heed my warning.
I come from a long line of heroes:

Isaac the Great, who could eat
an entire brisket at one sitting;
Seymour the Accursed, whose stories

had no beginning and no end;
Herschel the Terrible, who took
all comers at mah-jongg;

Stanley the Proud, renowned
for his hand-eye coordination;
the Long Arm of Aaron;

and my rumpled uncle Saul,
Liberator of Wind—warriors each
in their own way.

The chopped liver exudes an ill-starred augury,
pocked with portents of diced boiled egg,
which only a trained haruspex such as I can read.

I am as prescient as a glass display case,
as weather-wise as a prune sibyl
but will you listen? Will you learn?

Francine Rubin

Circle Dancing

My grandfather began dancing – *Bo Nepagesh,*
Hatsel Veani, Cheruti – his feet stepping lightly across
a wooden floor, his body moving in tandem
with other bodies. Linked by hands, each dancer
sustained the shape of cycle, perfection, reminders.

The refrains rang of a place my grandmother
had never visited but dreamt of – *next year in Jerusalem* –
said so adamantly in prayers, invoking a future
easier than the past – a childhood in tenement housing,
a middle age caring for children in a world
which sometimes didn't bend.

The dancing became a prayer too – a way to trace
the path, step by step, back to the beginning of the circle;
a way to find her memory; a way to merge
with other bodies in this life – feel their skin upon his skin,
the downbeat of their limbs, the rhythms of their corps
as they passed through song and time.

Carly Sachs

Talmud Study

How do you measure anything—
count your deaths, who loves you, who loves you not.
Today you are the ox, tomorrow the victim
of the gorging ox.
You build a house, you are holy,
but your walls are shaky.
Inside there is wine to be drunk.
Outside there is a plague.
You are on the wrong page.

Someone is coming to town on a donkey.
He will insult your intelligence
then ask for forgiveness.
Everything is a ratio, parts of the whole.

You watch the ants as they crawl across your plate.
You snuff out every third one with your pinky finger.
Years later they will say, *blood, frogs, boils,*
but what are they remembering?
Your house is falling—
who is the protagonist and what is it that he wants?

Michael Salcman

Sitting Shmira

Outside the morgue on First
and Thirtieth street, a canopy
has been erected next to
three truckloads of mixed body parts.
Under the tent, teams of young
yeshiva girls
sit shmira, watching over the dead
in four-hour shifts.
What should take only a day
has gone on for eight or nine weeks.
Since no one knows
who's in these trucks,
all the dead cops, candy vendors,
bond traders and unsuspecting passersby,
all the uncommon inhabitants
of our one earth's island
are assumed converted by fire and ash
into one Jew, one blood, and one flesh.
Since no one can be buried like this,
no one can be properly mourned.
But hour after hour, the sweet melodies
of psalms rise over the conversos
until a light is lit in David's garden,
a moon with a broken edge,
its author as anonymous as any victim.

Philip Schultz

Yom Kippur

You are asked to stand and bow your head,
consider the harm you've caused,
the respect you've withheld,
the anger misspent, the fear spread,
the earnestness displayed
in the service of prestige and sensibility,
all the callous, cruel, stubborn, joyless sins
in your alphabet of woe
so that you might be forgiven.
You are asked to believe in the spark
of your divinity, in the purity
of the words of your mouth
and the memories of your heart.
You are asked for this one day and one night
to starve your body so your soul can feast
on faith and adoration.
You are asked to forgive the past
and remember the dead, to gaze
across the desert in your heart
toward Jerusalem. To separate
the sacred from the profane
and be as numerous as the sands
and the stars of heaven.
To believe that no matter what
you have done to yourself and others
morning will come and the mountain
of night will fade. To believe,
for these few precious moments,
in the utter sweetness of your life.
You are asked to bow your head
and remain standing,
and say Amen.

Ken Seide

Lockdown Friday

When the lockdown lifted
I unlocked the door
stepped down the steps
walked down the walk
and
rediscovered the world
like a mourner rising from shivah

or
like Noah stepping down from the ark
into an empty world where nothing moved
except clouds and ripples on the water

I could have walked to the store
to see if it had opened
to see if it had hallah to sell
to see another person

Shabbat wouldn't come
for an hour and a half more
But I walked back inside
because I was
accustomed to the ark

*Poet's note: On Monday, April 15, 2013, two bombs exploded near the finish line of the Boston Mara-
thon, killing three people and injuring hundreds. On Thursday night of that week, two bombing suspects
killed a police officer and hijacked a vehicle. Those crimes led to a car chase, a firefight, and a manhunt
in Watertown, Massachusetts, and a lockdown on Friday, April 19 in areas near Watertown, including
Boston. People were ordered to shelter in place. Public transportation stopped and most businesses closed.*

Mark Everet Siegel

lamentations

i am my beloved's
and my beloved's mine
why must i wander
among the apple trees
chanting silver, gold, and purple
nigun of kaddish
not sung before to her
this anniversary of wedding nights

spiced wine
from my broken cup
spills
on the grass
of her new grave
later
i leave a stone
and three evening stars

Matthew E. Silverman

Pittsburgh on October 25, 2018 at 9:54 a.m.

The suspect in the deadly Pittsburgh Synagogue shooting has been charged with 29 counts of
federal crimes and weapon offenses after bursting into the Tree of Life Congregation Synagogue in
the Squirrel Hill neighborhood, yelling "All Jews must die."

I was thinking this morning about those moments,
Those little moments when we move and make a decision,
Which begin with a thought
That floats for an instant,
Lifts up like bird wings
Brightening the sky above
Everything grounded and hard and livable.

        Then I hear about a man who makes a decision,
        Causes those moments to fall fast, to turn
        Everything soft and wicked and unbearable.

Today, October is nearing an end.
The birds are flying farther South.
Already the November cold creeps in.
I should be shopping for the week,
Enjoying a venti cappuccino
Or watching an X-Men movie with my daughter,
While an electric heater purrs in the background.
So why is this Saturday different from all other Saturdays?

Instead, we learn the language of bullets,
A moment that makes us pay attention
Because we are drawn to sirens and sparks
The way a crowd turns toward
A firecracker show or how we bend our heads
Toward the traffic wrecks, craning
For the hint of death because we are human
And awed by the broken, the debris
Of lives scattered on asphalt and grass.
For some, this is a trophy case,

A display of words, stories told and retold
The way our ancestors told and retold epic poems around a fire.

Listen, they say, Jews control the world,
The media is leashed like a dog,
And financial companies make secret deals
In Yiddish. Universities wearing hidden *yarmulkes*,
Pushing propaganda from the Jewish puppet masters
Who chant: All hail Israel! All hail the Jew!
Read the Web for it tells the Truth about the Jewish lies,
Those weak, little, horned demons. "The Jews must
die! The Jews must die!"
And on they go: hate,
Hate, hate, hate.
As the Polish proverb goes:
If there is a problem, the Jews must be behind it.

Did you hear the one about the two Jews?
They went to an Internet café to peruse the headlines
In New York City (or Vienna if you prefer the 1930s version).
The taller one is reading the Yiddish news,
While the shorter one scans the latest propaganda. "Why
Are you reading that filth?" The shorter one shrugs his shoulders,
Puts down his bagel and shmear, leans
Back and says, "I used to read the Yiddish papers,
But *oy vey*!, all that suffering,
So much suffering!
Now, I read we control the world. I prefer
The good news!"

Oy, here is the Truth: the *Hibiscus trionum* blooms
Briefly and then the snow-colored petals twinkle
To time or wind, fading until nothing remains
When someone passes by the Flower-of-an-Hour
And remembers it was once summer and that it shall be
Summer once again. As he hurries home,
His earbuds recite the day's news.

> "These incidents usually occur
> In other cities,"
> Reports Wendell Hissrich, Pittsburgh
> Public Safety Director.

You might think this man walking home, minding
Himself, steady in the evening, to feel
Overwhelming sadness, and if this were a movie,
Rainfall would glisten his zipped jacket.
But he's indifferent, except to the cold whispering
Behind his ears that also wraps his nose
With numbness. What's on his mind?
He wishes for a long scarf and thick gloves.

Fall came early. The day ends
Before anyone is ready.
This single man, member of Generation Y,
Moves through the daily routine
Of work, home, work,
Even on a Saturday. Recently,
He let in a bob-tailed cat
With dark gray stripes who he lets
Lick the last slice of microwave pizza.
He half-watches a police drama on Netflix.
He thinks nothing of it.

> Today, a man so filled with hate,
> Killed. There's no other way to say it.
> It should never be necessary to say this.
> And yet we must give it a name,
> And name it often: evil.

Before bed, he washes and considers
The woman from work who hums childish tunes
And sighs twice near the end of her work shift,
As she rubs the small, silver bracelet in a circular motion
Around her wrist. He never asked what she thinks during this ritual
And so never knew her first born died young
During an unfortunate "accident," a crossfire.

Even though they work next to each other,
They never speak the blues or anything but the weather.
Around her neck, she wears a simple but elegant gold cross.
Sometimes she puts it in her mouth
To work through a particularly tough problem.
He watches this habit; she seems to be almost
Consuming the trouble.

In the mirror, he sees his own
Silver chain within the nest
Of his dark chest. He thinks nothing of evil
Or hate, and since it does not fall on his doorstep,
He gives it no thought.

Climbing into bed,
He fluffs a queen-sized pillow
And puts his back to it.
Opening to the beginning of the latest thriller,
He skims through the prologue,
Holding it between his thin arms,
Arms that desire to hold
This distant woman from work,
Hold her and stroke her hair,
Hair always wrapped like a hidden present,
Until there's no space left for wind,
Just warmth, a shadowing warmth
To light this sleepless night.

Melanie H. D. Sirof

Shiva

1.
Someone must return to the house first.
Someone must boil the egg
and place the water on the porch,
cover the mirrors
and unwrap the fish.
Someone must prepare the house
For absence.

2.
Like Escher's hands
we draw ourselves
into being, create
what is necessary
at the moment it is necessary.

If only we could draw the dead back,
reassemble
the wreck, and watch
them rise from the field
unharmed.

3.
We sit uncomfortably
close to the earth,
beards untamed, count
the missing,
the life they will miss.

4.
We correct the tense
of our verbs.
Speak as though they are
photographs.

5.
Remove the bookmark,
toothbrush,
glasses from the nightstand.
Check the calendar,
adjust the guest list,
imagine the falling.

6.
The house settles,
shrinks
to fit
the whole,
redefines itself
before the mourners.

7.
begins with a walk
around the block.
Slow, communal
as if to say
you are not alone

as if to say
you can go now
away from the home
where you grew.

As if to say
life is life and
not over.

Seven begins with
a walking away
and ends with a return.
Someone must walk away,
someone must return,
a walking away
a return.

Myra Sklarew

When He Lay Her Down

When the bully lay her down
upon the earth and brought his fists
to bear upon her child's body, when

he gathered her flailing wrists
like the delicate bones of birds and pinned
her down—did she exist

in his eyes? When he uttered
the dangerous words—Jew Jew—
she was not sure of her sin

for she had barely grown into
her Jewish skin. She lay
between a world she had newly

come to love—a simple classroom—
and a world she could not yet imagine
where years later she would resurrect

her bully, grant him immortal status—
his fists, the force of his anger,
hunkered down on a thin sheet of paper.

Amy Small-McKinney

Prayer

...may my life always bring honor to their memory
          from *Yizkor service*, Gates of Repentance

Because black bivalves filter out filth from polluted waterways.
Because they sieve away gallons of water a day.
Because we fed our rivers that fed its mussels enough
toxins to murder them all.
Because with dams taken down they might reproduce nonetheless.

Because the opening of the Altaussee Salt Mine where Nazis hid stolen art
glances out from a mountain named Loser and the mine continues nonetheless
to produce its brine.

Because blackness sucks me inside/closes over   no way out/ none I can see
ask why slashes separate one from another like half-closed doors.

Because we are separate and still there's prayer, dumb hope.

So I pray while pumping gas while noticing a crack in the hubcap
notice a $4.00 breakfast of coffee and bun and because I have no choice
listen to the blare from inside someone's car that shuts out my prayer then
          opens
it again busting into the world like Brahms' *discordant irregularities* and that is
          prayer's
paradox: it annihilates, it lifts—annihilates the other while lifting
          me up
into a false sky blue not blue but a shapeshifter trickster broken tongue
that tries to coax me/sell us—solid members of *a middle class who are now the
          poor with better credit*—faith in heaven only one way up.

I pray on the toilet to blue birds and jutting tan branches my dead mother
          framed
pray for chipped dishes to dead grandmothers their dishes white with gold
          flecks
or while waiting for blood to become water and suds. Last night

with fist over heart I thumped for each sin I know I sin though I'm not always
sure when or where. For that I am sorry.

For the blue jellyfish that are not jellyfish but colonies of polyps washed up on
        a cold shore though
I don't know why
I apologize to them or for breathing and war.

Though I'm not always kind to my husband or child
so late at night alone and remorseful stuff inside like stolen art hidden in a
        mine
crackling chips or creamy cookies it's funny it's not.

Because food and anger are the bounty I covet when the hole inside becomes
a trench so deep I feel my ancestors' bones, could fall into myself, not return.

When I am drowning in a river of not-forgiving.

I pray nonetheless to the middle-of-the-night blanket bloodied
with my husband's pain pray to escape Nebuchadnezzar's furnace alive intact
        amazed.

O blood O chips O hubcap O gas tank O toilet
remember the mighty mussels and salt mine that surprise even me.
Pray/notice/remember homes burned to the ground or flooded without arks
in our country of bitterness, we wait for the other shoe to drop.

Katherine Smith

Shepherd

The neighborhood shines before dark
like a child whose parents have properly taught her
the limits of the world, the small beauty

of whirring air conditioners, newspapers
carefully gathered from driveways Sunday mornings,
then refolded at dusk, the last sun on the white

blankets of the appaloosas grazing in the field.
You hope you have taught your daughter enough
about the temperature of grilled meat, about evenings

too cool for bare skin, about what one human
can be for another. Once you two lived
the only Jews for fifty miles

in a small town in Tennessee.
You hope you taught her well enough
how to read the book of the world

and not be haunted by its strangeness.
The swing-set has almost vanished.
On your evening walk, you dream that the night

about to fall on the neighborhood
has tangled in your daughter's hair.
You wake to a sharp bark from the white muzzle

of the Shepherd that, young, used to rush towards you,
teeth snapping. Now her grizzled tail glints, wagging,
as she herds you back to the friendly road.

Nomi Stone

Parable

They want to know if I know
Tom Cruise and I want to know how to ask
if they are upset that a girl may not speak
to a boy until he makes her a woman.

The sun is glowing hard on dusty streets
and whiter homes. The fox asked the fish,
why not live on land if you fear the fisherman?
In this example, they are the fish. Their holy book,
water.

Marcela Sulak

Better to Be Smart than Right

To get here today I had to wait at home
while Dr. Dalia Marx explained her interesting
theory that Israeli motherhood begins
with what the father is willing
to sacrifice, in women's poetry, because the phone
was plugged into the wall, recharging
the battery. To get here today was easy
compared to getting here last week

when I missed the bus
by five minutes because
I couldn't find the phone
and waited in the sun
reading poems about Sukkot,
forgiveness, and Yom
Kippur by depressing Israeli holocaust
survivors or children of holocaust

survivors or those expelled from Bagdad,
Aleppo, Cairo or Salonika and their sons
who fought in serial wars. Today I had
to face the wrath of my daughter's prin-
cipal, and the wrath of the disgraced
woman we'd thought to hire for native-
English speakers and who called me a back-
stabbing bitch on Facebook

when we did not hire her, though
my friend said her daughter liked her,
she herself might question
the propriety of 10-year-olds
writing about Jack-the-Ripper.
Since it was just before Yom Kippur,
we wrote a nice note to the principal,
to clarify that we thought well

of her teaching. Getting here today
it seems there are more mistakes
than not-mistakes, though this bus
has finally arrived, and with brakes
and wheels working, the card reader
beeping, and that mechanism
which distinguishes Jerusalem

money from that of Tel Aviv, and bus
money from train, the back-door closing
when it ought, and the driver having
obviously found his sun glasses,
an ironed shirt, belt, driver's license,
and managed to shave without cutting
himself. I wonder how often
he hears *It's better to be smart*

than right, and if it's as often
as I do. I am reading about
the production of space when
we get to the place soldiers get
off. The tall, slender one—
who floated on like a kite
is still adrift but displaying no
anger when the driver scolds

him for failure to show his ID
—is asking directions of civilians.
The woman beside me is sniffling,
I think she might be crying.
Let him go I mutter, in case
she needs some advice.

Philip Terman

Isaiah at Rest

All day I've been reading Isaiah,
Who I imagine to be ordinary,
In love with a woman who like you

Grows then cooks the vegetables
And only cares about a happy life.
Ye shall be confounded by the gardens

That ye have chosen doesn't apply to her,
He meant it in a more rhetorical way.
And when he arrives home late, his voice

Gone, his throat aching, feet scarred
And scratched from all the hard roads,
She puts in front of him a bowl

Of last season's harvest: potatoes, tomatoes,
Carrots, onions, basil, fennel, dill.
It tastes in his mouth not as the tongue

Of fire devours the stubble
Or as the dry grasses sinketh down in the flame
But more flavorful of their earth

Than the live coals that touched his lips
And took away his iniquities. He loosens
The girdle of righteousness from his waist,

And takes off completely the girdle
Of faithlessness from his loins,
Being in any case more full

Of the knowledge of his sources.
All flesh is grass, he whispers
Into her ear and the smell

Of his fiery breath
Makes her ask him to whisper it
Again.

Lenore Weiss

Discovering Hungarian at West End Mall

1.
Up Radnoti Miklos utca,
street named after the Hungarian poet
who died in labor camps months before liberation
in a city that volunteered Jews to Nazi death
ancestral home to parents who squeezed their way
past two World Wars to meet in New York City's immigrant hot-house.

I am looking to answer a question I have carried in a stone sack
within me for years, ransack a pastry shop and allow
poppy seeds, sugar, and lemon peel to fill my mouth, and like a moth
drawn to the lightest of things move toward West End Mall's three floors
of stores sit next to a statuesque ice-cream cone adorned with a red cherry
finish pastries and watch men and women belong to each other as I

try to break the code of this strange language
whispered in infant ears.

2.
Near the Chain Link Bridge
I wear a badge of pure white,
a strand that expanded to a tell-tale swatch,
my grandmother Lenke's mark on me,
not the yellow star pinned to a sleeve.

She escaped and entered Ellis Island
pregnant with my Aunt Clara, bastard child
who revealed the secret on her death bed,
how Lenke was

banned to the United States
to give birth, her sister's bindle
tucked inside a sewing machine.
Lenke's parents saved three lives, not their own.

They say by the time she reached 30
her hair gleamed as white as enamel,
and when she baked, she set out her cakes
with cloth and napkins.

I looked for her, my namesake,
my missing chain link
suspended over the Danube
running down my spine

and when the pot-bellied waiter
at the restaurant
came to my side and winked twice,
my mouth opened in Hungarian,
and he knew what I wanted.

Jane Yolen

Shoes: Holocaust Museum, Washington D.C.

I walk with foreknowledge into the museum,
sure it has nothing to teach me.
I've read the biographies, watched the movies,
sat through *Shoah* three times, *Schindler's List*.
I've touched a weeping stone in Heidelberg
for a synagogue set alight by hate;
interviewed Survivors; dated a survivor's child;
did the research; listened to a friend retell his childhood
in a Polish labor camp, forced to dive into the midden,
whenever the commandant's car drove by.

So why now, standing by a pyramid of shoes,
from a liberated camp,
am I stunned, undone, incapable of moving on?
Is it the sheer number of shoes in the pile
or the one on the top exactly the size
of my granddaughter's foot?

Elaine Zimmerman

Hostage

for Charlie Hebdo & the grocery victims

When memory and promise are one
facts tack on like hangers and nails.
Fibs become lies. Lies become
blankets. Everyone is lying down.

In Paris, weathered vanes and eaves
point south. Geese letter the sky.
A son bikes home a basket of candles,
quince and fresh marzipan.

When memory and promise are one
trees shake down small boys.
The sleepless start laughing.
What rattles a thin-boned cage?

When memory and promise are one
dogs bark on, as if locked in warning.
The family's front porch seems long
gone, but poke a thin joke slowly.

She irons a long gray dress.
The heat hides lies and wrinkles in
a complex time. Memory is a lost
silk slip, as winds turn a restless hunger.

When memory and promise are one,
sharp hymns tear the skin.
The kosher store means nothing at all
until they call it the Jewish store.

Then the shooting begins.
Nailed to memory, blankets of promise.
The joke is in the basket.
Everyone is lying down.

About the Editors

Nancy Naomi Carlson is a poet, translator, essayist, and editor, and has authored 10 titles (6 translated). *An Infusion of Violets*, her second full-length poetry collection, was published by Seagull Books (2019), and named a "New & Noteworthy" title by the *New York Times Book Review*. A recipient of grants from the NEA, Maryland Council for the Arts, and Arts & Humanities Council of Montgomery County, her work has appeared in such journals as *APR*, *The Georgia Review*, *The Paris Review*, and *Poetry*. She recently was decorated by the French government with the French Academic Palms and is a professor of graduate counseling at Walden University. Her website is www.nancynaomi-carlson.com.

Matthew E. Silverman teaches at Gordon State College and he is editor of *Blue Lyra Press*. His books include: *The Floating Door* (Glass Lyre Press) and *The Breath before Birds Fly* (ELJ Press). His poems have appeared in over 70 journals, including: *Crab Orchard Review, 32 Poems, December, Chicago Quarterly Review, North Chicago Review, Hawai'i Pacific Review, The Southern Poetry Anthology, The Los Angeles Review, Mizmor L'David Anthology: The Shoah, Many Mountains Moving, Pacific Review*, and other magazines. He co-edited *Bloomsbury's Anthology of Contemporary Jewish American Poetry* with Deborah Ager, and the forthcoming anthology: *New Voices: Contemporary Writers Confronting the Holocaust* with Howard Debs.

Contributors' Notes

Marjorie Agosín, a Chilean-American poet, novelist, and human rights activist, has been recognized by the United Nations with the Human Rights Leadership Award, and by the Chilean government with the Gabriela Mistral Prize. She is also a poet laureate for the Harvard Refugee Trauma Program. She is the author of more than fifty books that include narrative poetry, theatre and memoirs. Her acclaimed young-adult novel *I Lived on Butterfly Hill* was the winner of the Pura Belpré Prize. Marjorie teaches Spanish at Wellesley College where she holds the Luella Lamer Slaner professorship in Latin American Studies.

Patricia Averbach's poetry chapbook, *Missing Persons* (Ward Wood Publishing, 2013) won the London based Lumen/Camden prize and was cited by the *Times of London Literary Supplement* (November, 2014) as one of the best small collections of the year. Her debut novel, *Painting Bridges* (Bottom Dog Press, 2013) was praised by Michelle Ross, book critic for the Cleveland Plain Dealer, as "an introspective, intelligent and moving novel." Her second work of fiction, *Resurrecting Rain,* was published by Golden Antelope Press in December, 2019. She's a past director of the Chautauqua Writers Center in Chautauqua, New York.

Wendy Barker's seventh full-length collection of poems, *Gloss*, is forthcoming in 2020 from St. Julian Press. Her sixth collection, *One Blackbird at a Time* (BkMk Press, 2015), received the John Ciardi Prize. Her fifth chapbook is *Shimmer* (Glass Lyre Press, 2019). Other books include *Far Out: Poems of the '60s,* (co-edited with Dave Parsons, Wings Press, 2016), *Poems' Progress* (Absey & Co., 2002), and a selection of co-translations, *Rabindranath Tagore: Final Poems* (Braziller, 2001). Her poems have appeared in numerous journals and anthologies, including *The Best American Poetry 2013*. Recipient of NEA and Rockefeller fellowships, she teaches at UT San Antonio.

Helen Bar-Lev was born in New York in 1942. She holds a B.A. in Anthropology, has lived in Israel for 48 years and has had over 100 exhibitions of her landscape paintings, 34 of which were one-woman shows. She illustrated her six poetry collections. She is the Amy Kitchener senior poet laureate and was nominated for a Pushcart Prize in 2013. She is the recipient of the Homer European Medal for Poetry and Art. Formerly Assistant President of Voices Israel, Secretary, Chief Editor of Voices Annual Anthology, she now holds the title of Overseas Connections Coordinator. She lives in Metulla, Israel. Her website is www.helenbarlev.com.

Dara Barnat is a poet and researcher, who divides her time between Tel Aviv and New York. She completed her PhD on Whitman's influence on Jewish American Poetry at Tel Aviv University, where she teaches presently. *In the Absence*, Dara's first full-length collection of poetry, was released in 2016, and her chapbook, *Headwind Migration*, in 2009. Poetry, translations from Hebrew, and essays appear in *Shofar: An Interdisciplinary Journal of Jewish Studies*, *Washington Square Review*, *Los Angeles Review of Books*, *Poet Lore*, and elsewhere. Her poetry has been translated into Hebrew and French. Her work can be found at darabarnat.com.

Aliki Barnstone is a poet, translator, critic, editor, and visual artist. She is the author of eight books of poetry, most recently *Dwelling* (Sheep Meadow, 2016). She translated *The Collected Poems of C.P. Cavafy* (W.W. Norton, 2006). Among her awards are a Senior Fulbright Fellowship in Greece, the Silver Pen Award from the Nevada Writers Hall of Fame, a Pennsylvania Council on the Arts Fellowship in Poetry, and residencies at the Anderson Center and the Virginia Center for the Creative Arts. She is Professor of English at the University of Missouri and served as poet laureate of Missouri (2016-2019).

Tony Barnstone teaches at Whittier College and is the author of 20 books and a music CD, *Tokyo's Burning: WWII Songs*. His poetry books include *Pulp Sonnets*; *Beast in the Apartment*; *Tongue of War: From Pearl Harbor to Nagasaki*; *The Golem of Los Angeles*; *Sad Jazz*; and *Impure*. He is also a co-translator of Chinese literature, anthologist, and world literature textbook editor. Among his awards: The Poets Prize, Grand Prize of the Strokestown International Poetry Contest, Pushcart Prize, John Ciardi Prize, Benjamin Saltman Award, and fellowships from the NEA, the NEH, and the California Arts Council. His website is https://www.whittier.edu/academics/english/barnstone.

Ellen Bass is a Chancellor of the Academy of American Poets. Her most recent book, *Indigo,* was just published by Copper Canyon Press. Her poems appear frequently in *The New Yorker, American Poetry Review,* and many other journals. She coedited the groundbreaking anthology of women's poetry, *No More Masks!* and her nonfiction books include *The Courage to Heal: A Guide for Women Survivors of Child Sexual Abuse*. Bass founded poetry workshops at Salinas Valley State Prison and the Santa Cruz, California jails, and teaches in the MFA writing program at Pacific University.

Dan Bellm has published four books of poems, most recently *Deep Well* (Lavender Ink, New Orleans, 2017) and *Practice* (Sixteen Rivers, San Francisco), which won the 2009 California Book Award. Recent books of poetry in translation include *Speaking in Song,* by Mexican poet Pura López Colomé (Shearsman, UK, 2017) and *The Song of the Dead*, by French poet Pierre

Reverdy (Black Square, New York, 2016). He lives in Berkeley, California, and teaches translation and poetry at Antioch University Los Angeles. His website is www.danbellm.com.

Jill Bialosky is the author of four books of poetry, most recently, *The Players*, three novels, most recently, *The Prize* and two memoirs, NYT Bestseller, *History of a Suicide: My Sister's Unfinished Life* and *Poetry Will Save Your Life*. Her poems and essays have appeared in *The New Yorker, Paris Review, Atlantic,* and *Best American Poetry*. She was honored for her contribution to poetry by the Poetry Society of America in 2014. She lives in New York City.

Linda Blachman's book, *Another Morning: Voices of Truth and Hope from Mothers with Cancer,* is available from Seal Press. Recent work weaves Jewish content, themes and sensibility with an in-depth study of psychological and spiritual growth, grounded in personal experience. *Sarah Unbound* emerged from a four-year journey exploring the genesis, impact and healing of individual and generational trauma. Linda initially presented the *midrashic* poem on Rosh Hashanah at Congregation Netivot Shalom in Berkeley, CA, where she is a long-time member. She continues to work as a certified life transitions coach and trained facilitator of Wise Aging groups. Her website is www.lindablachman.com.

Michele Bombardier's collection, *What We Do,* is a finalist for the Washington Book Award. Her poetry is widely published in journals such as *Alaska Literary Review, Atlanta Review, Bellevue Literary Review* and others. She is a Hedgebrook fellow and the founder of Fishplate Poetry (fishplatepoetry.com) that offers workshops and retreats while raising money for humanitarian relief.

Bruce Bond is the author of twenty-three books including, most recently, *Sacrum* (Four Way, 2017), *Blackout Starlight: New and Selected Poems 1997-2015* (L.E. Phillabaum Award, LSU, 2017), *Rise and Fall of the Lesser Sun Gods* (Elixir Book Prize, Elixir Press, 2018), *Dear Reader* (Free Verse Editions, 2018), *Frankenstein's Children* (Lost Horse, 2018), *Plurality and the Poetics of Self* (Palgrave, 2019), and *Words Written Against the Walls of the City* (LSU, 2019). Presently he is a Regents Professor of English at the University of North Texas.

Pia Borsheim, Fredericksburg, VA. BA, MA: Eastern Michigan University. Ph.D.: Michigan State University. Professor of English, Gallaudet University, Washington, DC. Poetry books: *Moon on the Meadow: Collected Poems 1977-2007*, Gallaudet University Press, 2008; *Two Winters*, Finishing Line Press, 2011; *Mother Mail*, Hermeneutic Chaos Press, 2017; *Love Poems*, Cherry Grove Press, 2018. Recent journals: *storySouth, Southern Review, Northeast Narrative, Barrow Street, Tar Heel, Gulf Stream, Valparaiso Review, Michigan Quarterly Review*.

Leah Browning is the author of six chapbooks including *Orchard City*, a collection of short fiction published by Hyacinth Girl Press in 2017. Her fiction and poetry have appeared in *Mojave River Review*, *Four Way Review*, *The Forge Literary Magazine*, *The Threepenny Review*, *Valparaiso Fiction Review*, *Watershed Review*, *Superstition Review*, *The Homestead Review*, *Newfound*, *Clementine Unbound*, *Belletrist Magazine*, *Poetry South*, *The Stillwater Review*, and elsewhere. Browning's work has also appeared on materials from Broadsided Press and Poetry Jumps Off the Shelf, with audio and video recordings in The Poetry Storehouse, and in anthologies including *The Doll Collection* from Terrapin Books.

Doritt Carroll is a native of Washington, DC. She received her undergraduate and law degrees from Georgetown University. Her poems have appeared or are forthcoming in *North American Review*, *Coal City Review*, *Poet Lore*, *Rattle*, *Gargoyle*, *Nimrod*, and *Cherry Tree*, among others. Her collection *GLTTL STP* was published by Brickhouse Books in 2013. Her chapbook *Sorry You Are Not An Instant Winner* was published in 2017 by Kattywompus. She has been nominated for a Pushcart Prize and Best of the Net and works as a poetry editor for *The Baltimore Review*.

Laura Cesarco Eglin is the author of five collections of poetry, including *Calling Water by Its Name*, trans. Spanbauer (Mouthfeel Press), *Reborn in Ink*, trans. Kercheval and Jagoe (The Word Works), and *Occasions to Call Miracles Appropriate* (The Lune). Her translation of Hilda Hilst's *Of Death. Minimal Odes* (co•im•press) is the winner of the 2019 Best Translated Book Award in Poetry. Her poems and translations (from the Spanish, Portuguese, Portuñol, and Galician), have appeared in many journals, like *Modern Poetry in Translation*, *Eleven Eleven*, *Copper Nickel*, *Spoon River Poetry Review*, *Arsenic Lobster*, *International Poetry Review*, *Tupelo Quarterly*, *Columbia Poetry Review*, *Timber*, *Pretty Owl Poetry*. She is the publisher of Veliz Books.

Alex Cigale's first full book, *Russian Absurd: Daniil Kharms, Selected Writings*, came out in the Northwestern University Press World Classics series in 2017. In 2015, he was awarded an NEA Fellowship in Literary Translation. His own poems in English have appeared in *The Colorado Review*, *The Common Online*, and *The Literary Review*, and translations of classic and contemporary Russian poetry in *Harvard Review Online*, *The Hopkins Review*, *Kenyon Review Online*, *Modern Poetry in Translation*, *New England Review*, *TriQuarterly*, *Two Lines*, *Words Without Borders*, and *World Literature in Translation*. He recently edited the Russian issues of the *Atlanta Review* and *Trafika Europe*.

Stephen Cramer's first book of poems, *Shiva's Drum*, was selected for the National Poetry Series. *From the Hip*, his third book, follows the history of hip-hop in a series of 56 sonnets. *Bone Music*, his sixth collection, won the Louise

Bogan Award and was published by Trio House Press. His work has appeared in journals such as *The American Poetry Review, African American Review, The Yale Review,* and *Harvard Review*. An Assistant Poetry Editor at *Green Mountains Review*, he teaches writing and literature at the University of Vermont and lives with his wife and daughter in Burlington.

Carol V. Davis is the author of *Because I Cannot Leave This Body* (Truman State University Press, 2017), *Between Storms* (TSUP, 2012) and won the 2007 T.S. Eliot Prize for *Into the Arms of Pushkin: Poems of St. Petersburg*. Her work has been read on Radio Russia, National Public Radio and at the U.S. Library of Congress. Twice a Fulbright scholar in Russia, she teaches at Santa Monica College and Antioch University Los Angeles, and winter 2018 taught in Siberia.

Charles Dobzynski was born in Warsaw in 1929. His family emigrated to France the following year. In Paris, they escaped deportation during the Nazi occupation by living in hiding, in a basement—later to be the subject of a collection of Dobzynski's poems. He began to write and publish in his teens, first for the Résistance, then for literary journals, encouraged by Paul Éluard and Louis Aragon. He was the author of over 25 collections of poems, and the editor and translator of the Gallimard anthology of Yiddish poetry. He died in 2014.

Sharon Dolin is the author of six poetry collections, most recently *Manual for Living* (Pittsburgh, 2016), *Serious Pink* (Marsh Hawk, 2015 reissue), *Whirlwind* (Pittsburgh, 2012), and *Burn and Dodge* (Pittsburgh, 2008), winner of the AWP Donald Hall Prize for Poetry, as well as a translation of Gemma Gorga's *Book of Minutes* from Catalan (Field Translation Series: Oberlin, 2019). Her other awards include the Witter Bynner Fellowship, Fulbright Scholarship, Pushcart Prize, Drisha Arts Fellowship, and translation grants from PEN and Institut Ramon Llull. She is Associate Editor at Barrow Street Press and directs Writing About Art in Barcelona each June.

Moshe Dor (1932-2016), born in Tel Aviv, Israel, authored 40 books of poetry, essays, interviews and children's books. A recipient of the Bialik Prize, Israel's top literary award, he also served as Counselor for Cultural Affairs in London, and Distinguished Writer in Residence at American University, Washington, DC. In addition to being a journalist and radio personality, he was also a prolific translator with his own poems translated into 30+ languages as well as translating/editing into English numerous anthologies of contemporary Israeli poetry. He also wrote the lyrics of *Erev Shel Shoshanim* (Evening of Roses), performed worldwide as a wedding song.

Erika Dreifus, born in Brooklyn and raised there and in New Jersey, earned undergraduate and graduate degrees, including a PhD in history, from Harvard University, where for several years she taught history, literature, and writing. She is the author of *Birthright: Poems* (Kelsay Books) and *Quiet Americans: Stories* (Last Light Studio). Erika currently lives and writes in New York; her online home is https://www.erikadreifus.com/.

David Ebenbach is the author of seven books of poetry, fiction, and non-fiction, including the poetry collections *Some Unimaginable Animal* (Orison Books) and *We Were the People Who Moved* (Tebot Bach), as well as *The Artist's Torah* (Wipf & Stock), a non-fiction guide to creativity. He lives with his family in Washington, DC, where he teaches creative writing and literature at Georgetown University. You can find out more, if you like, at davidebenbach.com.

Dina Elenbogen, a widely published and award-winning poet and prose writer, is author of the memoir, *Drawn from Water: An American Poet, an Ethiopian Family, an Israeli Story* (BkMKPress, University of Missouri) and the poetry collection, *Apples of the Earth* (Spuyten Duvil, New York.) She has received fellowships from the Illinois Arts Council and the Ragdale Foundation and her work is forthcoming or has appeared in numerous anthologies and magazines including *Lit Hub*, *Bellevue Literary Review*, *Prairie Schooner*, *Poet Lore*, *December*, *Woven Tale Press*, *Paterson Literary Review* and many other venues. She has a poetry MFA from the Iowa Writer's Workshop and teaches creative writing at the University of Chicago Writer's Studio.

Eli Eliahu's publications include *Epistles to the Children*, (Tel Aviv: Am Oved Publishers, 2018); *Ir veh-beh-helot* [*City and fears*] (Tel Aviv: Am Oved Publishers, 2011), and *Ani veh lo malakh* [*I, and not an angel*] (Tel Aviv: Helicon, 2008). He is the recipient of the 2019 Brenner Prize for poetry, as well as the Matanel Prize for Young Jewish Writers (2013) and the Israel Prime Minister's Prize in Poetry (2014), and works as an editor at the daily *Ha-aretz*.

Julie R. Enszer is a scholar and poet. She is the author of four collections of poetry, *Avowed*, *Lilith's Demons*, *Sisterhood*, and *Handmade Love*. She is editor of *The Complete Works of Pat Parker*, winner of a Lambda Literary Award for Lesbian Poetry, and *Milk & Honey: A Celebration of Jewish Lesbian Poetry*, a finalist for the Lambda Literary Award in Lesbian Poetry. She is the editor of *Sinister Wisdom*, a multicultural lesbian literary and art journal, and a regular book reviewer for the *Lambda Book Report* and *Calyx*.

Pamela Hill Epps' work has appeared in literary publications such as *The Sandhill Review*, *Poetica*, *Wild Violet*, in *Writing Motherhood* (Scribner), and a chapbook, *A Last Glance*, published by Yellow Jacket Press. She is a psychologist, poet, and jazz musician living in Tampa, Florida with her partner and two cats. She spends a great deal of time looking out at the river.

Maia Evrona is a poet and prose writer, as well as a translator of Yiddish literature. Her poetry has received a Fulbright Scholar Award to Spain and Greece, while her translations of Yiddish poetry have received fellowships from the National Endowment for the Arts and the Yiddish Book Center. Her own original poetry has been published, in her own English to Yiddish translation, in the anthology *Radiant Jargon; Six Poems about Yiddish*. Her poems, as well as excerpts from her memoir on chronic illness, have also appeared in *Prairie Schooner*, *North American Review* and elsewhere.

Andrew Field is a poet and librarian living in Cleveland Heights, OH. He has published poems with *Mantis* and *Ocean State Review*, and is an active member of Infinite Conversations, an online forum with fun and wide-ranging discussions on poetry, literature, spirituality, and beyond. In 2016, his chapbook, *All I Want*, was published by Red Flag Poetry. He has a new manuscript, *Briefly, Suddenly, Longingly, Lovingly*, which he is currently sending out. The poem in this anthology was written during a fellowship with the Jewish Arts and Culture Lab, a program in Cleveland for Jewish artists and poets to explore Jewishness and Judaism through lectures, readings and discussions.

Hilene Flanzbaum is a literary critic, non-fiction writer, poet and professor at Butler University in Indianapolis. The granddaughter of Russian-Polish immigrants, she knows that history and her Jewish ethnicity are crucial to what she thinks and how she feels about living in this world.

Diane Frank is author of seven books of poems, two novels, and a photo memoir of her 400 mile trek in the Nepal Himalayas, *Letters from a Sacred Mountain Place*. Her new book of poems, *Canon for Bears and Ponderosa Pines*, was published by Glass Lyre Press. *Blackberries in the Dream House*, her first novel, won the Chelson Award for Fiction and was nominated for the Pulitzer Prize. Diane lives in San Rafael, where she dances, plays cello, and creates her life as an art form. She performs with the Golden Gate Symphony in San Francisco. Her website is www.dianefrank.net.

Jeff Friedman's newest book, *The Marksman*, will be published by Carnegie Mellon University Press in fall 2020. He is the author of seven previous poetry collections, including *Floating Tales* and *Pretenders*. Friedman's poems, mini stories and translations have appeared in *American Poetry Review*, *Poetry*, *New England Review*, *Poetry International*, *Hotel Amerika*, *The Bloomsbury Anthology of Contemporary Jewish Poetry*, *Flash Fiction Funny*, *Flash Nonfiction Funny*, *Fiction International*, *New World Writing*, *Imagining the Jewish God*, *The New Republic* and numerous other literary magazines. He has received numerous awards and prizes including a National Endowment Literature Translation Fellowship in 2016 and two individual Artist Grants from the New Hampshire Arts Council.

Alice Friman's seventh collection, *Blood Weather*, is from LSU. Her last two books are *The View from Saturn and Vinculum*, for which she won the 2012 Georgia Author of the Year Award in Poetry. Other books include *Inverted Fire* and *The Book of the Rotten Daughter*, both from BkMk, and *Zoo*, Arkansas, which won the Sheila Margaret Motton Prize from New England Poetry Club and the Ezra Pound Poetry Award from Truman State. A recipient of a Pushcart and included in *Best American Poetry*, she is Professor Emerita of English and creative writing at the University of Indianapolis and now lives in Milledgeville, Georgia, where she was Poet-in-Residence at Georgia College.

Joanna Fuhrman is the author of five books of poetry, including *The Year of Yellow Butterflies* (Hanging Loose Press, 2015) and *Pageant* (Alice James Books, 2009). Her poems have appeared in numerous journals, including *The Believer, Conduit, Fence, New American Writing,* and *Volt* as well as in various anthologies, including *The Pushcart Prize 2011* and *365 Poems for Every Occasion (*Abrams, 2015). She also creates poetry videos and teaches creative writing and multimedia composition at Rutgers University.

Joy Gaines-Friedler's works include three books of poetry, *Like Vapor, Dutiful Heart* and *Capture Theory* (2018 Foreword Review Book of The Year Finalist). She is a multiple Pushcart Prize nominee and featured in *The Bloomsbury Anthology of Jewish American Poetry.* Joy has awards from, among others, *Ekphrastic Magazine, The Litchfield Review, The Patterson Review,* The Tom Howard Prize, and The Marjorie Wilson Award for Excellence in Poetry. Joy holds an MFA in Creative Writing and teaches for non-profits in the Detroit area including literary arts programs, social justice organizations, and the Prison Creative Arts Project through the University of Michigan. Her website is www. joygainesfriedler.com.

Vladimir Gandelsman is the 2011 recipient of Russia's highest award for poetry, The Moscow Reckoning. Living in New York and St. Petersburg, he is the author of eighteen poetry collections, one verse novel, several important translations into Russian that include *Macbeth*, and a volume of collected works.

Robert L. Giron is the author of four collections of poetry; his poetry has appeared in national and international anthologies, including *Lovejets: Queer Male Poets on 200 Years of Walt Whitman, Knocking on the Door of the White House: Latino and Latina Poets,* and *Universal Oneness Poetry Anthology*, as well as in journals. He is also the editor of award-winning poetry anthologies and a co-editor of a women's studies anthology. He founded *The Sligo Journal* at Montgomery College and is the editor-in-chief of *Arlington Literary Journal (AtLiJo)* and publisher of Gival Press.

Barbara Goldberg has authored six prize-winning books of poetry, including *The Royal Baker's Daughter*, winner of the Felix Pollak Poetry Prize (University of Wisconsin Press). Her work appears in *Best American Poetry*, *Paris Review*, *Poetry*, *The Gettysburg Review* and elsewhere. Books translated and edited with Israeli poet Moshe Dor include *After the First Rain: Israeli Poems on War and Peace*. Goldberg received two fellowships from the National Endowment for the Arts as well as awards from PEN's Syndicated Fiction Project and Columbia University's Translation Center. She is Series Editor for the International Editions at The Word Works. Goldberg lives in Chevy Chase, Maryland.

Janlori Goldman's poetry collection, *Bread from a Stranger's Oven*, is published by White Pine Press (2017). Gerald Stern chose her poem "At the Cubbyhole Bar" for the 2012 Jewish Currents Raynes Prize. Goldman's poetry has been widely published, and she has written essays on Alicia Ostriker's poetry and Barbara Hammer's films. She teaches at Columbia and NYU, works at the Center for Justice, and volunteers as a writing mentor at MSKCC. Goldman received an MFA from Sarah Lawrence College. Her website is http://www.hugeshoes.org.

Ivonne Gordon Carrera Andrade, from Quito, Ecuador, is a widely anthologized international award-winning poet, literary critic, translator, and Professor of Spanish and Latin American Literature. She has published more than ten books of poetry and groundbreaking work about Nobel Prize winner, Gabriela Mistral. She has been the recipient of many international and national awards. As a Fulbright Senior Research Scholar, she worked on *The Trouble of Travels: Jewish Diaspora in Ecuador*. She has read at the Library of Congress, as well as many important international poetry festivals. Her work has been translated into English, Polish, Flemish, Romanian, and Greek.

David Greenstone is a trial lawyer and a poet. His poetry has been published in *Poetica Magazine, Blue Lyra Review* and *The Mizmor L'David Anthology*. He is also co-author of the book *Appropriate Apothejims: A Collection for Life*. David was born and raised in Dallas, Texas, where he still lives with his wife and their three daughters. He graduated from the University of Texas in 1995 with a BA in Government and Philosophy. He obtained his JD from the University of Texas School of Law in 1998.

Roger Greenwald attended The City College of New York and the Poetry Project workshop at St. Mark's Church In-the-Bowery, then completed graduate degrees at the University of Toronto. He has won two CBC (Canadian Broadcasting Corp.) Literary Awards (for poetry and travel literature), the Gwendolyn MacEwen Poetry Prize, and many awards for his translations from Scandinavian languages. He has published two books of poems: *Connecting Flight* and *Slow Mountain Train*. A third book is forthcoming.

Marilyn Hacker is the author of fourteen books of poems, including *Blazons* (Carcanet 2019), *A Stranger's Mirror* (Norton, 2015) and *Names* (Norton, 2010), and an essay collection, *Unauthorized Voices* (Michigan, 2010). Her sixteen translations of French and Francophone poets include Vénus Khoury-Ghata's *A Handful of Blue Earth* (Liverpool, 2017), Rachida Madani's *Tales of a Severed Head* (Yale, 2012) and Emmanuel Moses' *Preludes and Fugues* (Oberlin, 2016). She received the 2009 American PEN Award for poetry in translation for Marie Etienne's *King of a Hundred Horsemen,* and the international Argana Prize for Poetry from the Beit as-Sh'ir / House of Poetry in Morocco in 2011. She lives in Paris.

Gili Haimovich is an Israeli author and translator of Hebrew and English. She's the winner of the Osiaa di Sepia International Contest for best foreign author (Italy, 2019), and an excellency grant from the Israeli Ministry of Culture (2015), among other prizes. She has published six volumes of poetry in Hebrew, two chapbooks in English (*Sideways Roots* and *Living on a Blank Page),* and a multilingual book *(Note).* Her poems have been translated into about 30 languages, including a book in Serbian. Her first full-length English book, *Promised Lands* (Finishing Line) is forthcoming, together with her book *Hum,* translated into French (Jacques André Éditeur).

Edward Hirsch, a MacArthur Fellow, has published ten books of poems, including *The Living Fire* (2010), *Gabriel:A Poem* (2014), which won the National Jewish Book Award, and *Stranger by Night* (2020). He has also published five prose books, among them *How to Read a Poem and Fall in Love with Poetry* (1999), a national bestseller. A longtime teacher, at Wayne State University and in the Creative Writing Program at the University of Houston, Hirsch is now president of the John Simon Guggenheim Memorial Foundation. He lives in Brooklyn.

Jane Hirshfield's ninth poetry collection is *Ledger* (Knopf, 2020). She is author as well of two now-classic books of essays, *Nine Gates* and *Ten Windows,* and four books collecting world poets from the past. Honors include fellowships from the Guggenheim and Rockefeller foundations, NEA, and Academy of American Poets, and the Poetry Center and California Book Awards. A chancellor emerita of The Academy of American Poets and member of the American Academy of Arts & Sciences, Hirshfield's work appears in *The New Yorker, The Atlantic, The TLS, The Paris Review, Poetry,* and ten volumes of *The Best American Poetry.*

Paul Hostovsky is the author of ten books of poetry, most recently, *Late for the Gratitude Meeting* (Kelsay Books, 2019). His poems have won a Pushcart Prize, two Best of the Net awards, the *Comstock Review*'s Muriel Craft Bailey

Award, and the FutureCycle Poetry Book Prize. He has been featured on Poetry Daily, Verse Daily, and 21 times on The Writer's Almanac. He makes his living in Boston as a sign language interpreter and Braille instructor. His website is paulhostovsky.com.

Andrew Janco has co-translated, with Olga Livshin, the work of Russian-language poets ranging from Anna Akhmatova to Anastasia Afanasieva. Their translation work appears in numerous journals and anthologies, including *Words for War: New Poetry from Ukraine* and *Russian Contemporary Poetry: An Anthology*. He holds a PhD in Russian history from the University of Chicago and works as a digital scholarship librarian at Haverford College.

W. Luther Jett is a native of Montgomery County, Maryland and a retired special educator. His poetry has been published in numerous journals as well as several anthologies. He is the author of two poetry chapbooks: *Not Quite: Poems Written in Search of My Father*, released by Finishing Line Press in 2015, and *Our Situation*, released by Prolific Press in 2018.

Zilka Joseph was nominated twice for a Pushcart prize. Her work has appeared in *Poetry, Poetry Daily, Frontier Poetry*, *Kenyon Review Online*, *MQR*, *Asia Literary Review*, *Cha*, *Review Americana, Gastronomica,* and *Cheers To Muses: Contemporary Works by Asian American Women*. Her chapbooks, *Lands I Live In* and *What Dread,* were nominated for a PEN America and a Pushcart award respectively. *Sharp Blue Search of Flame,* her book of poems published by Wayne State University Press was a finalist for the Foreword Indies Book Award. She teaches creative writing workshops, and is a freelance editor and manuscript coach. Her website is www.zilkajoseph.com.

Marilyn Kallet is Knoxville Poet Laureate and the author, editor, or translator of 18 books, including *How Our Bodies Learned*, 2018, *The Love That Moves Me* and *Packing Light: New and Selected Poems*, Black Widow Press. Translations include Paul Eluard's *Last Love Poems* and Benjamin Péret's *The Big Game*. Dr. Kallet is Professor Emerita, University of Tennessee. Since 2009, she has led poetry workshops and writing residencies for the Virginia Center for the Creative Arts, in Auvillar, France. Recently she performed her poem, "Violins of Hope, Knoxville," with the Knoxville Symphony, at their program with violins rescued from the Holocaust.

Ilya Kaminsky is the author of *Deaf Republic* (Graywolf Press) and *Dancing in Odessa* (Tupelo Press). He has translated several books of poetry, most recently *Dark Elderberry Branch: Poems of Marina Tsvetaeva*, co-translated with Jean Valentine (Alice James Books), and co-edited several anthologies, including *Ecco Anthology of International Poetry*. He lives in Atlanta.

Jen Karetnick is the winner of the 2018 Split Rock Review Chapbook Competition for *The Crossing Over* (March 2019), as well as the author of eight other poetry collections, including *The Burning Where Breath Used to Be* (David Robert Books, 2020) and *The Treasures That Prevail* (Whitepoint Press, September 2016), finalist for the 2017 Poetry Society of Virginia Book Prize. Her work has appeared widely in publications including *Michigan Quarterly Review*, *The Missouri Review*, *North American Review*, *Prairie Schooner*, *River Styx*, *Salamander*, *Tampa Review*, and *Verse Daily*. She is co-founder/co-editor of the daily online literary journal, SWWIM Every Day. For more, see jkaretnick.com.

Gennady Katsov, a long-time Russian-American print and online (*Print Organ*, *Metro*, RUNYweb.com), radio (WMNB) and television (RTN) journalist, observer of both popular and high culture, and documentarian of the Russian émigré community in America, is the author of a book-length collection of ekphrastic poems, *Slovosphera*. Born in 1956 in Yevpatoria (Crimea), Katsov was one of the organizers of the legendary, unsanctioned, perestroika-era Moscow "Poetry Club" (1986). He immigrated to America in 1989. Katsov's more recent books, *Between Floor and Ceiling* and *365 Days Around the Sun*, were long-listed for the Russia Prize established by the Boris Yeltsin Fund to recognize the contributions to literature of the Russian diaspora.

Judith J. Katz is the Lead Teacher for Creative Writing at the Cooperative Arts and Humanities Magnet High School in New Haven, Connecticut, where her signature courses focus on writing poetry. Ms. Katz's work has been published in *The Muddy River Poetry Review*, *Crossing Class Anthology*, *Edify Fiction Literary Journal*, *Months to Years*, *The Literary Nest*, *Ritualwell*, *The Raven's Perch*, *The New Sound Literary Journal*, *Of Sun and Sand*, and *Sending Our Condolences*. She has been a first runner up in the "Kind of a Hurricane Press's Editor's Choice Awards" and recently won a NEH award to study Emily Dickinson.

Julia Knobloch was born and raised in Germany and has lived in France, Portugal, and Argentina. She is a former documentary filmmaker, a member of the Sweet Action poetry collective, and the recipient of a 2017 Brooklyn Poets Fellowship. Her debut collection *Do Not Return* was published in 2019 by Broadstone Books.

Nina Kossman is a Moscow-born painter, sculptor, poet, prose writer, and playwright. She is the author of two books of poems in Russian as well as the translator of two volumes of Marina Tsvetaeva's poems. Her other books include *Behind the Border* (HarperCollins, 1994), a collection of stories about her Moscow childhood; *Gods and Mortals: Modern Poems on Classical Myths* (Oxford University Press, 2001); and a novel. A collection of short stories in Russian is forthcoming.

Helene Seltzer Krauthamer has been writing poetry since she was in the third grade at P.S. 41 in the Bronx. She currently teaches English at the University of the District of Columbia. She thanks all who have encouraged and supported the arts and humanities.

Bruce Lader is the former Director of Bridges Tutoring, an organization educating multicultural students. His poems have appeared in *Poetry*, *The Bloomsbury Anthology of Contemporary Jewish American Poetry*, *Korean Expatriate Literature*, *Poetry Salzburg Review*, *New York Quarterly*, *Harpur Palate*, *The Einstein Journal of Biology and Medicine*, and other magazines. Lader's books include *Fugitive Hope* (Cervená Barva Press), *Embrace* (Big Table Publishing), and *Discovering Mortality* (March Street Press), a finalist for the 2006 Brockman-Campbell Book Award. A 2015 Pushcart Prize nominee, he won the international 2010 Left Coast Eisteddfod Poetry Competition and has received a writer-in-residence fellowship from The Wurlitzer Foundation.

Joy Ladin is the author of nine books of poetry, including Lambda Literary Award finalists *Impersonation* and *Transmigration*; a memoir, National Jewish Book Award finalist *Through the Door of Life: A Jewish Journey Between Genders*; and *The Soul of the Stranger: Reading God and Torah from a Transgender Perspective,* a Triangle and Lambda Literary Award finalist. Her honors include an NEA writing fellowship and a Fulbright Scholarship. She holds the Gottesman Chair in English at Yeshiva University. Her work is available at www.wordpress.joyladin.com.

David K. Leff is poet laureate of Canton, Connecticut, an award winning essayist, and former deputy commissioner of the Connecticut Department of Environmental Protection. He has authored six nonfiction books, three volumes of poetry and two novels in verse. In 2016-2017 the National Park Service appointed him poet-in-residence for the New England National Scenic Trail (NET). David has given nature poetry workshops at the famed Sunken Garden Poetry Festival, the Mark Twain House, the Emily Dickinson Museum, and elsewhere. David's journals, correspondence, and other papers are archived at the University of Massachusetts Libraries in Amherst. For more go to www.davidkelff.com.

Merrill Leffler has published three collections of poetry, *Partly Pandemonium, Partly Love*; *Take Hold;* and *Mark the Music*. In addition to translating with Moshe Dor *The Poetry of Eytan Eytan* for a special issue of *Shirim: A Jewish Literary Journal,* he has guest-edited several issues of *Shirim* and *The Changing Orders: Poetry from Israel* for *Poet Lore*. Leffler is the publisher of Dryad Press, which has been publishing books of poetry, fiction, and non-fiction since 1976. He lives in Takoma Park, Maryland, where he was the city's Poet Laureate from 2011-2018.

David Lehman is a poet, writer, and editor. Educated at Yeshiva Rabbi Samson Raphael Hirsch, Stuyvesant High School, Columbia and Cambridge universities, he is the author of ten books of poetry (most recently *Playlist*, 2009) and nine works of nonfiction (including *A Fine Romance: Jewish Songwriters, American Songs*, which won ASCAP's Deems Taylor Award). He is the editor of *The Oxford Book of American Poetry* and the founding and longtime series editor of *The Best American Poetry*. In fall 2019, Cornell University Press published his *One Hundred Autobiographies: A Memoir*, which centers on his bout with cancer.

Jeffrey Levine is the author of three books of poetry: *Rumor of Cortez*, nominated for a 2006 Los Angeles Times Literary Award in Poetry, *Mortal, Everlasting*, which won the 2002 Transcontinental Poetry Prize, and most recently, *At the Kinnegad Home for the Bewildered*, Salmon Press, 2019. Levine is Artistic Director and Publisher of Tupelo Press, an award-winning independent literary press. Also an accomplished musician, Levine is a concert clarinetist, jazz guitarist and pianist.

Matthew Lippman's collection *Mesmerizingly Sadly Beautiful* won the 2018 Levis Prize and will be published by Four Way Books in 2020. His recent collection, *A Little Gut Magic*, is published by Nine Mile Books. He is the Editor and Founder of the web-based project Love's Executive Order (www.lovesexecutiveorder.com).

Olga Livshin is the author of *A Life Replaced: Poems with Translations from Anna Akhmatova and Vladimir Gandelsman,* which considers immigration and translation during the Trump era. Her poetry and translations are published in the *Kenyon Review, Poetry International,* and other journals. She lives outside Philadelphia.

Dennis Maloney is a poet and translator. A number of volumes of his own poetry have been published including *The Map Is Not the Territory: Poems & Translations, Just Enough,* and *Listening to Tao Yuan Ming.* A bilingual German/English volume, *Empty Cup* was published in Germany in 2017. Recent collections include *The Things I Notice Now* and *The Faces of Guan Yin.* His works of translation include: *The Stones of Chile* by Pablo Neruda, *The Landscape of Castile* by Antonio Machado, *Between the Floating Mist: Poems of Ryokan,* and *The Poet and the Sea* by Juan Ramón Jimenez.

Irina Mashinski is the author of ten books of poetry in Russian. She is co-editor, with Robert Chandler and Boris Dralyuk, of *The Penguin Book of Russian Poetry* (Penguin Classics, 2015), and co-founder (with the late Oleg Woolf) and editor-in-chief of the *StoSvet/Cardinal Points* project. She is the recipient of several literary awards, and, with Boris Dralyuk, of the First Prize in the 2012 Joseph Brodsky/Stephen Spender Translation competition. Her first English-language collection, *The Naked World*, is forthcoming from Spuyten Duyvil. She has taught at New York University, Montclair State University, and New Jersey high schools.

Jed Myers is author of *Watching the Perseids* (winner of the Sacramento Poetry Center Book Award), *The Marriage of Space and Time* (MoonPath Press), and several chapbooks, including *Dark's Channels* (winner of the *Iron Horse Literary Review* Chapbook Award) and *Love's Test* (winner of the Grayson Books Chapbook Competition). Recent recognitions include the *Prime Number Magazine* Award for Poetry, *The Southeast Review*'s Gearhart Poetry Prize, and *The Tishman Review*'s Edna St. Vincent Millay Poetry Prize. Recent poems appear in *Rattle, Poetry Northwest, The American Journal of Poetry*, *Southern Poetry Review*, and elsewhere. He is Poetry Editor for the journal *Bracken*.

Yvette Neisser is the author of *Grip*, winner of the 2011 Gival Press Poetry Award. Her translations from Spanish include *South Pole* by María Teresa Ogliastri and *Difficult Beauty: Selected Poems* by Luis Alberto Ambroggio. Her poems, translations, essays, and reviews have appeared in such publications as *Foreign Policy in Focus*, *Virginia Quarterly Review*, and the *Bloomsbury Anthology of Contemporary Jewish American Poetry*. She is founder and co-director of the DC-Area Literary Translators Network (DC-ALT) and has taught writing at George Washington University and The Writer's Center. By day, she is a writer for an international development firm.

Leslie B. Neustadt, writer and visual artist, is a retired New York Assistant Attorney General and the author of *Bearing Fruit: A Poetic Journey*. Widely published, her work is illuminated by her Jewish upbringing and expresses her experiences as a woman, daughter, wife, mother, and cancer patient. Visit www.leslieneustadt.com.

Rachel Neve-Midbar's collection *Salaam of Birds* won the 2018 Patricia Bibby First Book Award and was published by Tebot Bach in 2019. She is also the author of the chapbook, *What the Light Reveals* (Tebot Bach, 2014). Rachel's work has appeared or is forthcoming in *Blackbird, Prairie Schooner* and *Georgia Review* as well as other publications and anthologies. She was recently a finalist for the COR Richard Peterson Prize, winner of the Passager Poetry Prize and nominated for The Pushcart Prize. Rachel is currently a doctoral candidate at the University of Southern California in Los Angeles. More at rachelnevemidbar.com.

Lesléa Newman has created more than 70 books for readers of all ages including the short story collection, *A Letter to Harvey Milk,* the poetry collections *I Carry My Mother, Lovely,* and *October Mourning: A Song for Matthew Shepard* (novel-in-verse) and the children's books, *A Sweet Passover; Runaway Dreidel!; Ketzel, The Cat Who Composed,* and *Gittel's Journey: An Ellis Island Story.* Her literary awards include poetry fellowships from the National Endowment for the Arts and the Massachusetts Artists Foundation, the Association of Jewish Libraries Sydney Taylor Award, two American Library Association Stonewall Honors, and the Massachusetts Book Award.

Jean Nordhaus' volumes of poetry include *Memos from the Broken World, My Life in Hiding, Innocence,* and *The Porcelain Apes of Moses Mendelssohn.* She has published work in *American Poetry Review,* the *New Republic, Poetry* and *Best American Poetry 2000* and *2007.* Her work was featured in *Innisfree Poetry Journal's* "A Closer Look," and on the poetrymagazine.com website. She previously served as poetry coordinator at the Folger Shakespeare Library, President of Washington Writers' Publishing House, and Review Editor of *Poet Lore,* the oldest continuously published poetry magazine in the U.S. She lives on Capitol Hill in Washington, DC.

Joshua Sassoon Orol is a trans Jewish poet from Raleigh, NC, writing with the texts, tunes, and stories passed down from their mixed heritage family. Joshua completed an MFA at North Carolina State University, and received an Academy of American Poets prize while at the University of North Carolina at Chapel Hill. Their poetry can be read in recent or forthcoming issues of *Mud Season Review, Nimrod,* and *Poetry.*

Leonard Orr has published three books of poetry: *Why We Have Evening* (2010), *Timing Is Everything* (2012), and *A Floating Woman (2015),* all from WordTech/Cherry Grove. His work has appeared in *Poetry International, Rattle, Black Warrior Review, Cirque,* and elsewhere. He is the author or editor of many critical books and teaches literature, critical approaches, and Representations of the Holocaust at Washington State University Vancouver.

Jacqueline Osherow was raised in Philadelphia, Pennsylvania. She received a BA from Harvard University and a PhD in English from Princeton University. She is the author of eight books of poetry, including *My Lookalike at the Krishna Temple* (Louisiana State University Press, 2019), *Ultimatum from Paradise* (Louisiana State University Press, 2014), *Whitethorn* (Louisiana State University Press, 2011), and *Looking for Angels in New York* (University of Georgia Press, 1988). Osherow has received the Witter Bynner Prize and fellowships from the Guggenheim Foundation, the Ingram Merrill Foundation, and the National Endowment for the Arts. She serves as a distinguished professor of English and creative writing at the University of Utah.

Alicia Ostriker has twice received the National Jewish Book Award for Poetry and has been twice nominated for the National Book Award, among other honors. As a critic she is the author of *Stealing the Language: the Emergence of Women's Poetry in America*, and other books on poetry and on the Bible, most recently *For the Love of God: the Bible as an Open Book*. Her most recent collections of poems are *Waiting for the Light* and *The Volcano and After*. She is currently the New York State Poet Laureate, and a Chancellor of the Academy of American Poetry.

Alan Michael Parker is the author of nine collections of poems, including *The Age of Discovery* (Tupelo Press, 2020), and four novels. Awards for his poetry include three Pushcart Prizes, two selections in *Best American Poetry*, the North Carolina Book Award, the Brockman-Campbell Award, the Medwick Award from the Poetry Society of America, and the Randall Jarrell Poetry Prize (in 2013, 2014, and 2019). Houchens Professor of English at Davidson College, he also teaches in the University of Tampa low-residency MFA program. He can be found at www.alanmichaelparker.com.

Linda Pastan has published 15 books of poetry, 2 of which were finalists for The National Book Award. The latest, *A Dog Runs Through It*, was published by Norton in 2019. She has won many awards, including the Ruth Lily Award for Lifetime Achievement. She is a former Poet Laureate of Maryland and for 20 years was on the staff of the Bread Loaf Writer's Conference.

Marge Piercy has published 19 poetry collections (recently *Made in Detroit* [Knopf]) as well as 17 novels, including *Sex Wars*. PM Press reissued *Vida* and *Dance the Eagle to Sleep,* and brought out *The Cost of Lunch, Etc.* (short stories) and *My Body, My Life* (essays, poems). She has read at over 500 venues here and abroad.

Susan Rich is the author of five books, most recently, *Cloud Pharmacy*, shortlisted for the Julie Suk prize, honoring poetry books from independent presses and *The Alchemist's Kitchen,* Finalist for the Washington State Book Award. She has been awarded a Fulbright Fellowship to South Africa, PEN USA Award for Poetry, and the Times (of London) Literary Supplement Award. Her poems have appeared in all 50 states including in the *Harvard Review*, *New England Review*, *O Magazine*, and *World Literature Today*. Her next book is *Blue Atlas*.

Alison Ridley teaches Spanish at Hollins University in Roanoke, Virginia. She received her doctorate from Michigan State University. Her scholarly research focuses on the theatre of Antonio Buero Vallejo. She has published articles and book reviews in various academic journals and a number of translations for Marjorie Agosín. Currently, Alison is translating two new works by

Marjorie: a collection of poetry and the sequel to the novel, *I Lived on Butterfly Hill*.

Kim Roberts is the author of *A Literary Guide to Washington, DC: Walking in the Footsteps of American Writers from Francis Scott Key to Zora Neale Hurston* (University of Virginia Press, 2018), and five books of poems, most recently *The Scientific Method* (WordTech Editions, 2017). She is the editor of two anthologies, *Full Moon on K Street: Poems About Washington, DC* (Plan B Press, 2010) and *O Say Can You See: The Early Poets of Washington, D.C.* (University of Virginia Press, forthcoming 2021), and she co-edits the web exhibit *DC Writers' Homes*. Her website is http://www.kimroberts.org.

Francine Rubin is the author of the chapbooks *City Songs* (Blue Lyra Press), *Geometries* (Finishing Line Press), and *If You're Talking to Me: Commuter Poems* (forthcoming from Dancing Girl Press). She is online at francinerubin.tumblr.com.

Carly Sachs is the author of *the steam sequence* and the editor of the anthology *the why and later*, a collection of poems about rape and assault. Her poems and stories have been included in The Best American Poetry Series and read on NPR's Selected Shorts. She writes, teaches yoga, and lives in Lexington, Kentucky.

Michael Salcman, poet and art historian, was chairman of neurosurgery at the University of Maryland and president of Baltimore's Contemporary Museum. Poems appear in *Arts & Letters*, *Hopkins Review*, *Hudson Review*, *New Letters*, and *Ontario Review*. His anthology of classic and contemporary poems on doctors, patients, illness and healing, *Poetry in Medicine*, appeared in 2015 (Persea). Salcman is the author of three collections, *The Clock Made of Confetti* (Orchises, 2007), nominated for The Poets' Prize, *The Enemy of Good Is Better* (Orchises, 2011), and *A Prague Spring, Before & After*, poems about the Shoah (Evening Street Press, 2016), winner of the 2015 Sinclair Poetry Prize.

Philip Schultz is the author of several collections of poetry, including *Failure*, winner of the 2008 Pulitzer Prize. His other collections include *Luxury*, *The Wherewithal: A Novel in Verse*, *The God of Loneliness: New and Selected Poems*, *Living in the Past*, and *The Holy Worm of Praise*. He has also published a memoir, *My Dyslexia*, in which he recounts his difficulties with the debilitating language disability and his struggles to overcome it. His work has been published in *The New Yorker*, *Partisan Review*, *The New Republic*, *The Paris Review*, *Slate*, and other magazines. He is the recipient of a Fulbright Fellowship, a Guggenheim Fellowship, and a National Endowment for the Arts Fellowship in Poetry. His website is https://blueflowerarts.com/artists/philip-schultz/.

Ken Seide is the pen name of a resident of Newton, Massachusetts. His poems have appeared in *Midstream, Poetica, Kerem, New Vilna Review, Voices Israel, Soul-Lit, SN Review, Whistling Shade, The Deronda Review, CCAR Journal: The Reform Jewish Quarterly, Napalm and Novocain, Rat's Ass Review / Love & Ensuing Madness*, and other journals. His short stories have appeared in *Poetica, Cyclamens and Swords, Pound of Flash*, and *Bindwood*. "Lockdown Friday" appeared in his chapbook *Tikkun Alef-Bet: Jewish Poems of Love, Loss, Hope & Holiness & Click Boom: Jewish Stories of Farce.*

Mark Everet Siegel is a retired Professor of Psychology. He has written and studied poetry for many decades. Publication had not been a priority but the inclusion of his poem in this anthology is appreciated. He plays and studies improvisational Spanish Flamenco and American blues. In 2014 he earned the rank of Shodan from the Japan Karate Association. He has been legally blind since age 12.

Melanie H.D. Sirof is a Brooklyn-born, suburbia-raised teacher, writer, and Jew. Molded in the early 90s by the mountains of Boulder, Colorado, Melanie's work is frequently influenced by mountains and canyons. References from a lifetime of High Holy Day services frequently surprise her by showing up in her poetry. She holds an MFA from Hofstra University where she received an Academy of American Poets University Prize.

Myra Sklarew studied biology at Tufts University, attended the Writing Seminars at Johns Hopkins, studied bacterial viruses and genetics with Max Delbruck and Salvador Luria at Cold Spring Harbor Biological Laboratory. In the fifties she worked at Yale Medical School studying delayed response memory and prefrontal cortex function. Professor emerita, American University, founder of the MFA Program in Creative Writing, and winner of the National Jewish Book Council Award in Poetry, she served as president of Yaddo Artists' Community. Poetry collections include *Harmless, Lithuania: New and Selected Poems;* prose, *Like a Field Riddled by Ants*; essays, *Over the Rooftops of Time. A Survivor Named Trauma: Holocaust Memory in Lithuania* is forthcoming from SUNY Press.

Amy Small-McKinney's poetry has been published in numerous journals such as *The Cortland Review, American Poetry Review, The Indianapolis Review, Connotation Press, LIPS, Tiferet Journal*, and elsewhere. Her second full-length book of poems, *Walking Toward Cranes*, won the Kithara Book Prize 2016 (Glass Lyre Press). Small-McKinney's reviews of poetry books have appeared in a number of journals, including *Tiferet, Connotation Press*, and *Prairie Schooner*. Her poems have also been translated into Romanian and Korean. Small-McKinney teaches community poetry workshops in Philadelphia. She has an MS in

Neuropsychology from Drexel University and an MFA in Poetry from Drew University.

Katherine Smith's publications include appearances in *Poetry, Cincinnati Review, Missouri Review, Ploughshares, Southern Review* and many other journals. Her short fiction has appeared in *Fiction International* and *Gargoyle*. Her first book *Argument by Design* (Washington Writers' Publishing House) appeared in 2003. Her second book of poems, *Woman Alone on the Mountain* (Iris Press), appeared in 2014. She teaches at Montgomery College in Maryland.

Scott Spanbauer teaches Spanish at the University of Colorado, Boulder. His translation of Uruguayan poet Laura Cesarco Eglin's collection *Calling Water by Its Name* was published by Mouthfeel Press in 2016, and his translation of Adolfo Pardo's *The Grill* by Veliz Books in 2017.

Nomi Stone is a poet and an anthropologist, and the author of two poetry collections, *Stranger's Notebook* (TriQuarterly 2008) and *Kill Class* (Tupelo 2019). Winner of a Pushcart Prize, Stone's poems appear recently in *POETRY, American Poetry Review, The New Republic, The Best American Poetry, Tin House, New England Review*, and elsewhere. She has a PhD in Anthropology from Columbia and an MFA in Poetry from Warren Wilson, and she is an Assistant Professor in Poetry at the University of Texas, Dallas.

Marcela Sulak's fourth collection of poetry, *City of Skypapers,* and first memoir, *Mouth Full of Seeds*, are forthcoming from Black Lawrence Press. Her five book-length translations include Karel Hynek Macha's *May* and K.J. Erben's *A Bouquet of Czech Folktales*, from the Czech, and from the Hebrew, *Twenty Girls to Envy Me. The Selected Poems of Orit Gidali* was nominated for the 2016 PEN Award for Poetry in Translation. For her current translation project, the poetry of Sharron Hass, Sulak received a 2018 National Endowment for the Arts Fellowship for translation. The co-editor of the 2016 Rose Metal Press title, *Family Resemblance: An Anthology and Exploration of 8 Hybrid Literary Genres*, Sulak is an Associate Professor of English at Bar-Ilan University.

Philip Terman's most recent collection is *Our Portion: New and Selected Poems*. A selection of his poems, *My Dear Friend Kafka*, has been translated into Arabic and published by Ninwa Press. His poems have appeared in numerous journals including *Poetry Magazine, The Kenyon Review, The Sun Magazine*, and *99 Poems for the 99 Percent*. He's a professor of English at Clarion University and is the coordinator of The Bridge Literary and Arts Center in Franklin, Pennsylvania. He has collaborated with other artists, including composers, painters, and sculptors, and performs his poetry with the jazz band The Barkeyville Triangle.

Lenore Weiss lives in Oakland, California, where she tutors middle and high school students in writing and reading comprehension. Her three poetry collections form a trilogy about being mortal: *Cutting Down the Last Tree on Easter Island* (West End Press, 2012), *Two Places* (Aldrich Press, 2014), and *The Golem* (Hadassa Word Press, 2017). She is currently at work on an environmental novel.

Mary Jane White is a retired trial lawyer who holds an MFA from the Iowa Writers' Workshop, and has been awarded two NEA Fellowships, one in poetry and one in translation. Her Tsvetaeva translations appear, along with early original poems, in *Starry Sky to Starry Sky* (Holy Cow! Press, 1988); in *New Year's*, an elegy for Rilke (Adastra Press, 2007); and in *Poets Translate Poets*, (Syracuse, 2013). *After Russia, Poem of the Hill, Poem of the End and New Year's, Poems of an Emigrant* (a bilingual text) is forthcoming in 2020 from Adelaide Books (NYC/Lisbon). Contact her at maryjanewhite@gmail.com.

Jane Yolen is the author of almost 400 published books, including 10 books of adult poetry. Her career spans children's books, Young Adult, adult publishing. Six colleges and universities have given her honorary doctorates for her body of work. She was the first writer to receive the New England Public Radio's Arts & Humanities Award, and the first woman to give the Andrew Lang lecture at St Andrews University in Scotland since the series began in 1927. She has three Holocaust novels out and a memoir in verse of her father's family's immigration from a shtetl in the Ukraine to America (1912-1914).

Elaine Zimmerman is a policy leader for children and poet. Her work is often democracy-focused. She helped in cultural and political activities in the first post-communist decade in Eastern Europe. In the United States, she created a multi-state democracy school for parents, the Parent Leadership Training Institute. Poetry appears in journals such as *Lascaux Review, Coal Hill Review, Lilith, Adanna Literary Journal, New Millennium, New Guard Literary Review, Cyclamens and Swords,* and anthologies including, *Forgotten Women, Everybody Says Hello, and Worlds in Our Words—Contemporary American Women Writers*. Honors include the Nutmeg, Connecticut Poetry, William Stafford, and a Pushcart nomination.

Glossary

Afoh at, Ema?: Hebrew for "Where are you, my mother?"

Aleph: first letter of the Hebrew alphabet

Aliyah: Hebrew term referring to being called to the podium in a synagogue to read from the Torah (Hebrew scriptures)

Bo Nepagest, Hatsel Veani, Cheruit: names of Israeli folk dances

Bracha: Hebrew for a blessing or benediction

Bubelah: Yiddish term of endearment (darling, sweetie), often used by Grandmothers when speaking to grandchildren

Daven: Yiddish term referring to praying, usually with a back and forth, swaying motion

Dunam: Hebrew term referring to a unit of land area equal to about one-quarter of an acre, especially as used in the state of Israel

Emeinu: Hebrew for "our mother"

Einzatsgruppen: German term referring to Nazi death squads

Frum: Yiddish for "religious, devout, pious," and generally used in the context of Orthodox Judaism

Halacha: Hebrew term referring to Jewish law that supplements scriptural law

Hineni: Hebrew for "Here I am," and is the response Abraham gave God when asked to sacrifice Isaac

Judía de mierda: Spanish ethnic slur to describe a Jewish person

Kippot (singular is **kippah**): Hebrew term referring to skullcaps or head coverings worn in synagogues as a sign of respect, though more observant Jews wear them daily (see *yarmulke*)

Lejana pero fuerte: Spanish for "distant but strong"

L'dor v'dor: Hebrew expression meaning "from generation to generation" and is an exhortation Jews receive regarding their responsibility to pass on their traditions and religion to the next generation

Makht zikh greyt tzu antloyfn: Yiddish for "get ready to run"

Mansy: Yiddish for "old wives' tales"

Meydeleh: Yiddish for "little girl"

Mentsch: Yiddish for a person of integrity, a "good" person

Mishpooha: Yiddish term used to describe the extended family, "the tribe"

Muy lejana: Spanish for "very distant"

Niddah: Hebrew term referring to the period of time when Jewish law forbids sexual relations, beginning with the first day of a woman's menstrual cycle and ending after she immerses herself in a ritual bath

Niggun/nigun: Hebrew term referring to a traditional Jewish folk melody or mystical musical prayer with no formal lyrics, but using vocalizations such as "Bim-Bim-Bam" and "Ai-Ai-Ai"

Nu es: Yiddish for "come on, eat"

Nyet: Russian for "no"

Oy vey!/Oy gevalt!: Yiddish interjection expressing distress, frustration, or grief

Porque así se hace los viernes: Spanish for "because that is how it's done on Fridays"

Que soy de herencia judía lejana: Spanish for "that I'm of distant Jewish ancestry"

Rachmones: Yiddish for compassion

Rafles: French term used to describe the roundup of civilians in German-occupied countries, who were then sent to labor camps, though Jews in hiding were often shot dead on the spot

Seylch: Yiddish for "sense"

Shim'i!: Hebrew for "hear!"

Shuk: Hebrew term for a street market in Israel

Sof Olam: Hebrew for "end of the world."

Tallit: Hebrew term for a Jewish prayer shawl whose fringes are meant to remind the wearer of the commandments of the Torah

Tekiah Gedolah: Hebrew term referring to the longest sound blown on a shofar (ram's horn),

T'rei: Hebrew for "you will see"

Tsurris: Yiddish for trouble, distress, aggravation

Volk: German term referring to people in a crowd or from one ethnic group

Yama (яма): Russian for pit

Yarmulke: Yiddish term referring to a skullcap or head covering worn in synagogues as a sign of respect, though more observant Jews wear them daily (see *kippot*)

Zayde, zaide: Yiddish for grandfather

מנין Hebrew for "minyan" referring to the requirement of a quorum of ten people (usually men) over the age of 13 to hold traditional Jewish public prayer

סרטן Hebrew for "cancer"

Acknowledgments

While there have been so many people who have helped bring this project to life, we'd be remiss if we didn't mention the invaluable contributions of certain individuals. We are eternally grateful to our contributors, without whom this anthology could not exist. We also wish to thank the wonderful editors at Ashland Poetry Press, Deborah Fleming and Jennifer Rathbun, who believed in our vision from the start. In addition, thanks go to Roger Greenwald and Jeffrey Levine for their editorial guidance; Catherine Maigret Kellogg for her formatting expertise; Marilyn Kallet and Alice Friman for helping to spread the word about our call for Jewish-themed poems; Lee Shapiro for her invaluable proofreading skills; Jody Sachs, metalsmith, who allowed us to use, for our cover, an image of the sterling silver Jewish-themed wedding ring she designed and crafted, titled "Your House is My House"; and to Claire Zoghb for lending us her artistic talents to come up with her superb cover design. Finally, we gratefully acknowledge the following literary journals and presses who generously gave us permission to reproduce their work:

Marjorie Agosín. "Entwined in your Silence" appeared in *Braided Memories* (Solis Press). Copyright © 2019. Translated by Allison Ridley. Reprinted with permission. All rights reserved.

Patricia Averbach. "My Father's Dream" appeared in *Missing Persons* (Ward Wood Publishing). Copyright © 2013. Reprinted with permission. All rights reserved.

Aliki Barnstone. "Name Change" appeared in *Dwelling* (Sheep Meadow Press). Copyright © 2015. Reprinted with permission. All rights reserved.

Wendy Barker. "Waking Over *Call It Sleep*" appeared in *One Blackbird at a Time: Poems by Wendy Barker* (BKMK Press). Copyright © 2016. Reprinted with permission. All rights reserved.

Ellen Bass. "Pines at Ponary" appeared in *The Kenyon Review*. All rights reserved.

Dan Bellm. "Counting" appeared in *Zeek*. All rights reserved.

Jill Bialosky. "They Came" appeared in *Ploughshares*. All rights reserved.

Bruce Bond. "Benthos" appeared in *The New South* and in *Choir of the Wells* (Etruscan Press). Copyright © 2013. Reprinted with permission. All rights reserved.

Leah Browning. "I Go Back in Time and Rescue My Mother" appeared in *Salome Magazine*. All rights reserved.

David Ebenbach. "While They Choose a New Pope, I Eat a Bagel" appeared in *Some Unimaginable Animal* (Orison Books). Copyright © 2019. Reprinted with permission.

Dina Elenbogen. "A Voice" appeared in *Poetica*.

Alice Friman. "Ammunition" appeared in *Blood Weather* (LSU Press) and in *The American Journal of Poetry*. Copyright © 2019. Reprinted with permission.

Vladimir Gandelsman. "Stills" appeared in *Eleven Eleven*. Translated by Olga Livshin and Andrew Janco.

Barbara Goldberg. "Furlough" appeared in *Tikkun*.

Janlori Goldman. "Yom Kippur" appeared in *Bread from a Stranger's Oven* (White Pine). Copyright © 2016. Reprinted with permission.

Marilyn Hacker. "Calligraphies II" appeared in *Blazons: New and Selected Poems 2000-2018* (Carcanet Press, UK). Copyright © 2019. Reprinted with permission.

Edward Hirsch. "A Small Tribe" appeared in *Literary Imagination*.

Jane Hirshfield. "My Confession" appeared in *The New York Review of Books* and in *Ledger* (Knopf). Copyright © 2020. Reprinted with permission.

Ilya Kaminsky. "Dancing in Odessa" appeared in *Dancing in Odessa* (Tupelo Press). Copyright © 2014. Reprinted with permission.

Joy Ladin. "A Modest Proposal" appeared in *The Future is Trying to Tell Us Something: New and Selected* (Sheep Meadow Press). Copyright © 2017. Reprinted with permission.

Merrill Leffler. "What I Want of It" appeared in *Mark the Music* (Dryad Press). Copyright © 2012. Reprinted with permission.

David Lehman. "A Modest Proposal" appeared in *Yeshiva Boys* (Scribner). Copyright © 2009. Reprinted with permission.

Olga Livshin. "Eating a Persimmon, 1954" appeared in *Matador Review*.

Dennis Maloney. Excerpt from "Border Crossings" appeared in *The Things I Notice Now* (MadHat Press). Copyright © 2018. Reprinted with permissions.

Jed Myers. "Jewish Cemetery Night" appeared in *Rattle*.